ASCENDING GROWTH

Improve Customer Value.

Drive Business Growth.

Elevate Your Career.

EVE CHEN,

LJUBICA RADOICIC,

& BRETT COWELL

Ascending Growth: Improve Customer Value. Drive Business Growth. Elevate Your Career.

REVOLUTIONAIR
ideas that change lives

Published by Revolutionair Publishing
4500 S Monaco Street, #1136
Denver, Colorado 80237

Copyright © 2022 Eve Chen, Ljubica Radoicic, Brett Cowell
First Publication 2022

Revolutionair and its logo are trademarks of The Growth Engine LLC. All other trademarks are the property of their respective owners.

A catalog entry for this book is available from the Library of Congress Cataloging-in-Publication.

ISBN: 979-8-88796-425-6

Edited by Gabrielle Gerbus
Back Cover Page Photo by Tony Pizzamiglio

DISCLAIMER

For all the pioneers who dare to do the hard work to ascend and create trails for those behind, we dedicate this book to you.

Acknowledgements

"If I have seen further, it is by standing on the shoulders of giants"
Isaac Newton

This book could not have been written without the giants in our orbits. We are filled with gratitude to step on the shoulders of these giants in order to ascend and we are committed to pay it forward by being the giants for others too.

First of all, it is impossible to extend enough thanks to our families, who gave us the love, encouragement, and support that we needed throughout the last three years while we worked on this book, as our world went through an unprecedented time during the covid-19 pandemic.

"To Maya, you are the motivation in my life that pushes me to be a better person everyday. To Erik, for standing by me and being my biggest cheerleader when I felt uncertain. To Ljubica and Brett, for your friendship and commitment on this journey with me. To my clients and former colleagues, for being open about the challenges we went through together and for your trust, willingness, and bravery to ascend with me. It was through the countless conversations we had that gave birth to some of the concepts in this book."
- Eve Chen

"To my family for their unconditional love and the sacrifices they made to support me on this journey. To the B2B marketing community in APAC who are the inspiration for this project. My quest to move marketing beyond a cost-center role and gain a seat at the leadership table resonated with so many marketers I met at various events and webinars. Seeing that we are on a similar journey inspired me to share my experience. This book is a way to say we're in this together and there is a better way." - Ljubica Radoicic

"For Darcy, Jack and Charlotte. I'd also like to acknowledge the following mentors who have been instrumental in my career and introduction to organizational transformation: Guy Ferrier, Peter Dowling, Ian "Fish" Fisher, Claus V. Jensen and Andrew Caveney." - Brett Cowell

We also want to express our deep and sincere gratitude to the following people without whom this book would not have come about:

To Archie Fraser, for bringing Eve and Ljubica together, it is your belief in "we are better together" and your collaborative approach in your leadership that gave birth to this book.

To all the people that were part of the writing and review process: Gabrielle Gerbus, Dietrich Bückner, Jade Meara, Carmel Mosser, Amanda Becker, Andrew Smith, Bernadette McClelland, Emma Robourgh, Prof. Dr. Marc Peter, Andrew Everingham, Jennifer Arnold, Natalie Truong, Mona Lolas, Hamish Thrum, Shahin Hoda, and Cheryl Hayman. You are the pioneers who are selfless to share your knowledge and experience and dare to be the leaders to change our community for the better.

Preface

On a hot summer day, a little over fourteen years ago, Ljubica and I met at a cool café in Sydney, Australia. A mutual friend had brought us together to compare notes about a new transformation project on which Ljubica was about to embark. I'd been working as the Head of Marketing for a multinational company and had just rolled out the organization's first global marketing automation software (MAS). After reading Steven Woods' book *Digital Body Language*, I had been inspired to start the MAS journey. Later, as the full reality of the challenge struck home, I started wondering what I'd gotten myself into! The tech was sexy and held so much promise, but my organization was far from ready.

Ljubica was working as the Head of Marketing for a global professional services company going through a period of heavy acquisitions. She had been brought in as a specialist to consolidate 11 brands under one umbrella and articulate the new brand value to clients, partners, and suppliers.

At the time, neither of us knew that this strategic chat would be the start of a decades-long friendship and collaboration.

As Ljubica recalls - "I left the meeting inspired by our conversation of how technology can enable marketers to show demonstrable ROI by developing integrated demand and lead generation programs, supported by sales enablement tools that take into consideration the buyer's journey. This was a novel concept at the time since the buyer's journey was moving to digital, and the industry I worked in was still traditionally focused on face-to-face engagements. I was keen to disrupt the status quo."

Fast forward to 2014. I'd ventured out of the world of enterprise and pursued my dream of becoming an entrepreneur. I had started a digital marketing agency that later transformed into a revenue marketing agency. I was working on the concepts behind the Revenue Generation Value Chain model that you'll read about in this book. Then, out of the blue, I got a phone call from Ljubica that left me sleepless for a couple of nights.

"Hey Eve, I am going to take my team and the entire company on a revenue generation transformation! Are you open to joining me on this journey?" she asked.

It took me around a month to decide to take on the challenge. Four days after joining, before I was even assigned a company laptop, I found myself on a plane to Manila with Ljubica to onboard a new marketing shared services team. During that 10-hour flight from Sydney to Manila, Ljubica went through some of the challenges ahead of us.

For the next 12 months, we would be tasked with transforming an organization that had been operating in a traditional industry for several decades. Marketing was viewed as a cost center and had been through major cuts.

No sweat, right?

But where would we even start?

With people.

And so, the adventure began.

You'll hear more about that transformation and the lessons learned from countless others throughout the book. More than a decade after our chat, we've stayed in each other's orbit despite living in different countries. Ljubica continued to ascend in her Marketing leadership journey, and I've built out my consulting practice. We continue to share notes on industry practice and 'marketing as a growth engine'.

In 2020, when the pandemic hit, there was a spike of interest in how to create business growth. Organizations and practitioners were looking for a structured and proven approach to help them handle business in a state of flux. Ljubica joined the speaking circuit presenting case studies of successful organizational transformations she delivered and showcased some of the frameworks I'd created. The overwhelming response from marketers inspired her to suggest that I compile the materials into a book!

The writing process soon saw us bringing in an old friend, Brett Cowell, who is an experienced management consultant, entrepreneur, and creative in his own right. After examining what we knew about *sustainable* growth across all our combined years of experience, a pattern emerged that successful and sustainable change in business inevitably required *three things* to converge.

The first of these things is *organizational growth* e.g., in terms of capability, maturity, and customer acquisition. Next comes *customer growth*, in terms of customers "winning" as a result of doing business with the organization. And finally, *people growth*, in terms of personal, leadership and career growth, and even purpose and self-actualization.

We soon began calling the intersection of these three areas the *Growth Experience*, or GX view. Once christened, GX began to take on a life of its own! It felt like we'd stumbled upon a name and frame to the thing for which every business leader was searching.

We hope that this book will provide you all that you need to grow. It remains a practical, principled, and structured guide to transforming business results, and in the process, transforming yourself.

The scope of this book, and the frameworks discussed within, are broad enough to facilitate discussion across different parts of the business to build a common vocabulary and approach to growth. Whether you're a marketer wanting to step up, or an executive wanting to lead organizational improvement, this book is for you.

We've been lucky to have great friends and colleagues that have helped us step up and conquer challenges we'd never have imagined. Reflecting on the impact of this support has led us to establish the greater goal of helping elevate marketers on a similar journey to ours. That is, a quest to embed marketing as a value and revenue generating function with a seat at the leadership table. We are hoping our work will help *elevate 1 million marketers* globally! Find out more about this at www.ascending-growth.com

We have been in the trenches for sure, but the journey has also been an adventure, and one that keeps generating new challenges and possibilities. Marketing has provided us with endless opportunities to grow both professionally and personally.

We hope to meet you out there (at least virtually) at a conference or event sometime. Until then, may this book be a conversation that makes a difference to your work and life.

With your success in mind,

Eve Chen,

Colorado, May 2022

CONTENTS

Introduction

"In growing companies, there is a surge of personal and collective energy. People live the intoxicating experience of being on a winning team."

The Alchemy of Growth

Have you ever watched a flock of birds swarm, bend, and soar at sunset? It's a magical sight. Similarly, we've seen cross-functional teams at leading organizations move as one, effortlessly and gracefully.

We've found time and again that success in business first and foremost comes because of *getting the right people aligned and working effectively.*

It is the premise of this book that you, the leadership team, and a "leveled-up" B2B marketing function, will be the driving force behind aligning the organization and building the culture required to support growth.

Despite this, Marketing is often sidelined or minimized in the exact types of organizations that need strong Marketing leadership the most. The Marketing team often has to justify its own existence, or is diluted as a subset of the Sales team, with no seat at the table, credibility, or significant voice.

CMOs are challenged to prove their value in a fast-changing environment, with boards and CEOs setting high expectations. Accenture's "CMO Insights" confirms that nearly one-third of CEOs are looking to their CMO to be at the helm of finding new growth sources. The 2021 CMO Survey by Deloitte, finds that 58.7% of Marketing leaders surveyed report increased pressure from CEOs, while 45.1% cite pressure from CFOs to prove the value of marketing. Yet CMOs have the shortest tenure of all C-suite board members and only 26% of them get regularly invited to board meetings!

Ongoing disruptions in the business environment are putting significant pressure on marketing departments.

Customer expectations are rising. Competitors are circling. Things can't carry on the way they are working. Organizations need to be better aligned, more responsive, more focused on the right things. You may find yourself wishing that someone would do something to change it. That person is you. It has always been you.

We're at an inflection point with technology like Artificial Intelligence (AI), Augmented Reality/Virtual Reality and even cryptocurrencies, which are already presenting further business opportunities, ethical challenges, and even social and *ecological* considerations.

Building trust in organizations and their leadership remains an imperative. Environmental and social issues such as climate change and income inequality are pressing. Customers and employees in both B2C and B2B want those they do business with to be working toward a greater purpose. On top of that, marketers are looking for meaningful ways to add value and connect with customers to deliver on the brand promise.

Marketing leaders need to navigate their organizations and careers with principle to create a better world. The line between work and personal life has blurred. As leaders *we* are looking for meaning, growth, community, and to contribute using whatever "levers" we can.

For the above reasons, we've structured this book as a principle-based leadership journey, more like a conversation than a textbook. Yes, we'll describe powerful models that you can use to transform the organization, but these must be filtered through your genuine desire to do the right thing and to win together with your colleagues, customers, and people.

* * *

Organizations want to improve and drive growth, but they often lack a compelling vision of the future, plan for integrating the right capabilities, or cultivate the ability to execute change. This results in piecemeal efforts and improvement projects that either fail or fail to deliver the intended benefits.

To address these obstacles and support your leadership journey, this book will address vision, blueprint, and execution through three major concepts, each having an associated framework.

Those are:

1. Sustainable growth is at the overlap of Organization, Customer/Market, and People
2. Grow results by optimizing the ten capabilities of the Revenue Generation Value Chain
3. If you're not Ascending, you're Descending

The associated frameworks for these concepts are:

1. Growth Experience (GX)
2. Revenue Generation Value Chain (RVC)
3. Ascending Growth Method (AGM)

Let's look at each idea and framework in more detail.

Major Concept 1: Sustainable growth is at the overlap of Organization, Customer/Market, and People

The first big idea is that there is a sweet spot for generating sustainable growth at the intersection of organizational, customer and people growth. We call this intersection Growth Experience or GX.

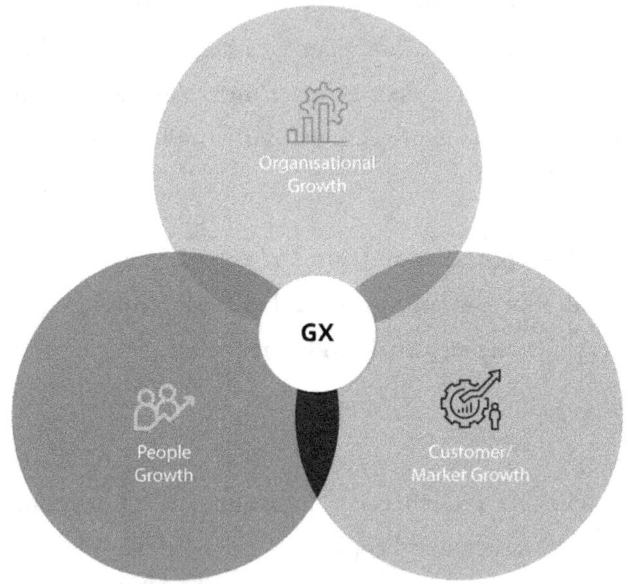

Illustration 1: Growth Experience (GX)

The principle behind GX is that there is a "win-win-win" opportunity at the center of the Venn diagram. Neglect any circle and the possibility of sustainable growth begins to wane (though short-term results might still be possible). Focusing on the intersection of all three is a powerful way to generate new growth ideas. GX represents a new paradigm, a new way of seeing.

After intense focus on CX (Customer Experience) during the pandemic, firms are now asking what's next? GX (Growth Experience) represents a more comprehensive vision and framework for customer and market growth drivers that is integral to delivering sustainable growth over time.

Let's discuss each circle more. At the Organizational level, external measures of growth include increases in revenue, customers, and profit. In our experience, growing revenue sustainably requires developing internal *capability*. This means doing the "right things the right way" in ten capability areas (see next section). GX will transform strategy, structure, skills, branding, and other critical capability areas.

Historically, the functional axis of power in B2B organizations has been Sales or Product/Engineering. However, GX presents the idea of breaking down silos and bringing the best of the organization to market in an integrated way. It also empowers Marketing to move beyond being a cost center or revenue generator to lead the entire organization toward a higher purpose. One that resonates with both internal and external stakeholders and supports sustainable growth.

The second circle starts with Customers. External measures of *Customer growth* in B2B include the increase in *customer's* revenue and lifetime value *to* customer, as well as the number and value of those customers.

The overlap between Organization and Customer is the value that your organization creates for the customer in addition to the value you create for the *people* within the customer's organization like leaders, buyers, and users.

In B2B, you'll likely deal with buying groups. Thinking about the value you provide the customer's team as well as the customer's organization will bring additional growth ideas.

If working with you and your firm makes customers' lives easier, then they're more likely to keep you around, become ongoing clients, and recommend you to others.

The second part of the Customer circle is *Market*, which refers to the industries/sectors your organization does business with now, or could in future, plus the detailed internal dynamics and characteristics of those markets.

As a Marketing leader, you'll be the oracle for customer and market knowledge within the organization. It's not enough to delight your *current* customers based on what they need *today*. Marketing will guide the organization to new markets and new customers, and deepening relationships with existing customers.

You have the opportunity to transform the role of Marketing from traditional brand steward to being the architect of organizational success.

We can change the customer conversation to be one about shared growth and create a pipeline of new customer and market ideas and opportunities.

The third circle is People Growth, which also has two interlinked parts. First is *your personal development journey* and effectiveness as a leader, and second is improvement in your team's independent and collective performance.

For example, measures of team outcomes could include:

- the results of culture or employee satisfaction surveys and turnover
- the number of new ideas submitted for product or continuous improvement
- the milestones around skills development e.g., training hours completed

We'd expect to see these increase because of a GX transformation.

Next in *People growth* is your own development as a leader.

Measuring leadership performance includes financial metrics (e.g., meeting or exceeding revenue targets, marketing ROI) as well as leadership effectiveness (e.g., 360-degree reviews, formal and informal feedback) that will show your growing skill as a leader.

We've taken great pains in writing this book to make it human and practical, and to avoid seeing B2B marketing as purely funnel optimization or a technology enablement project.

Instead of having a funnel as the top-level concept, we see GX as three complementary "orbits" (think electrons, moons, or planets). The customer/market orbit comprises a continuous cycle of Attraction i.e., Acquisition, Retention, and Expansion as shown in the diagram below.

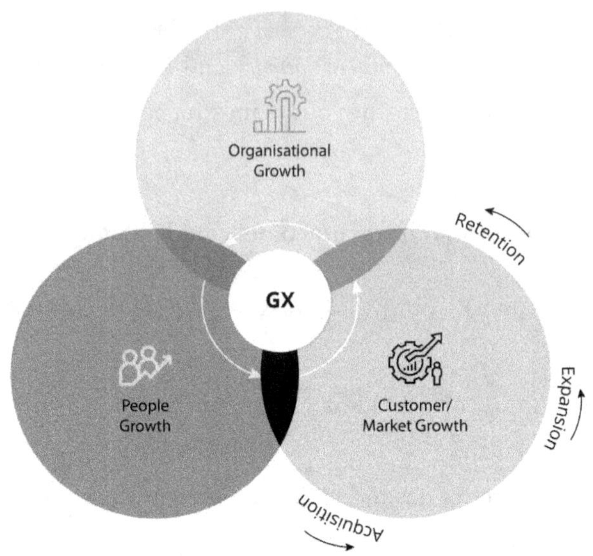

Illustration 2: Customer Orbit of Growth Experience (GX)

In GX, the organization tries to attract people and customers into its orbit.

Prospects move towards us because of what we do and who we are (including branding, mission). We move prospects into our orbit, satisfy them, and ultimately convert them into customers.

At moments where customers might otherwise drift away, we avoid complacency and act (using data and process to be proactive) to retain them. We help customers grow and our people grow. As a result, the scale and depth of our relationships with customers and our people increase.

Success is less like a moon shot, and more like a cyclical process that has its own positive momentum and is sustainable by becoming a virtuous cycle.

Major Concept 2: Grow results by optimizing ten capabilities of the Revenue Generation Value Chain (RVC)

Marketing and organization are a value chain comprising ten major components of organizational capability.

Each component represents an area of skill that the firm must further develop to support growth. For example, the firm must work on their Growth Strategy (Component 1) and Customer Knowledge (Component 2) as well as the other eight links in the chain to support growth.

The benefits of alignment are undeniable. Forrester research has shown that B2B organizations with well-aligned product, marketing, and sales functions experience 19% faster revenue growth and 15% higher profitability than those that are misaligned.

We call this aligned business model the *Revenue Generation Value Chain* or RVC (see diagram below). In addition to connecting internal activities of the firm, the RVC exists *externally* in the organization's brand and reputation as well as other environmental factors.

Here is what RVC looks like:

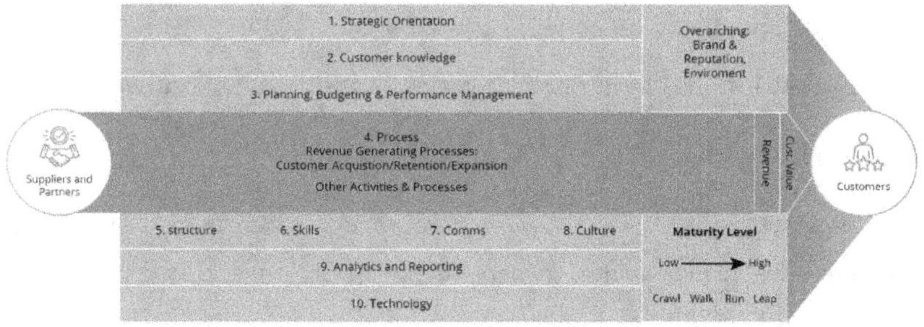

Illustration 3: Revenue Generation Value Chain (RVC).
For a larger version see the last page of this chapter

The crux of the RVC is highlighted in the shaded center. These are the same processes we've been talking about in GX: Customer Acquisition, Customer Retention, and Customer Expansion.

We want to optimize each of these processes individually and then make them operate as a continuous cycle or "orbit."

Using the RVC approach, we look *at everything the firm does* through the lens of how that contributes to driving revenue. We ask again and again; do we have the right people aligned and focused on the right things to drive revenue?

How about in your organization, are people aligned and working on the right things to drive revenue?

When starting to use the RVC model, the answer will inevitably be "no."

Like any modern organization, there will be a lot of busy people and frenetic activity, though it won't be clear how much of that activity contributes to revenue. The painful truth is that people are probably not only being pulled in different directions but also pointing in different directions and potentially even working on things that destroy revenue rather than enhance it.

The inspiration for the model came out of industry and client practice that led to conducting our own primary research in 2020.

The *2020 Growth Engine's Revenue Generation Maturity Study* surveyed respondent firms across ten dimensions of marketing/organizational capability and analyzed the correlation between capability levels and overall business results.

Capability was categorized into one of four levels, *Crawl, Walk, Run,* and finally *Leap,* based on criteria we've identified from industry and client experience. Overall capability was then assessed, and a comparison with planned and actual results made.

The research confirmed our practical experience, i.e., that firms with higher levels of the right capabilities had a greater chance of meeting or exceeding their revenue goals.

For us, this finding validated the RVC approach and the idea of using it as both an audit or assessment tool, and as a "blueprint" for designing how Marketing should work alongside the other functions and the organization to deliver sustainable growth in the future.

The RVC in its current form also builds on Michael Porter's value chain concept (e.g., *Competitive Advantage*), and updates it for the contemporary age.

That is, not only are Sales and Marketing *part* of what a firm does, but many firms *are* essentially Sales and Marketing organizations.

Other functions (e.g., production and engineering) are increasingly managed in regional or global service centers or outsourced to other firms.

Another perspective on the value chain is that customers are now increasingly favoring *better service* over incremental product/service features. So, the focus of value analysis (and incremental investment) should adjust accordingly to processes in the organization that drive better service.

Use the RVC to engage your organization and leadership team in discussion on how customers and markets have changed, and why we need to move on from previous assumptions and past organizational paradigms if we want to continue to compete and grow.

Major Concept 3: If you're not Ascending, you're Descending

We see organizations either *building momentum* and creating a *virtuous* cycle towards growth, or losing momentum and getting stuck in reactivity, resulting in being caught in a *vicious* cycle. The same applies to you in your role.

In a sense, if you're not *ascending* then you're *descending*.

Where does your organization sit in terms of momentum right now? Are you going up or down?

We've worked with organizations where the sense of shared ownership and responsibility for "winning together" is palpable. And this is not about winning once, but building a winning culture, and being proud to be on a winning team.

This doesn't happen overnight but is the result of developing creative confidence and an ability to get results, grow, and change.

Part of building that confidence comes from having a consistent approach to change. One that encompasses project management, change management, and benefits realization. We call our approach AGM (Ascending Growth Method), which comprises five stages: Align, Data, Design, Deploy and Sustain.

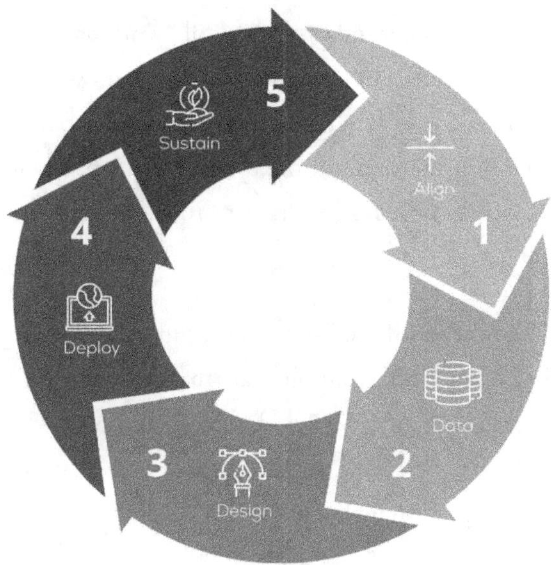

Illustration 4: Ascending Growth Method (AGM)

By using AGM, you'll align expectations over what needs to be done, gather data to analyze current issues and opportunities, and design the future blueprint for marketing to capture these opportunities and embed growth in the organization's DNA.

The final two stages of AGM, Deploy and Sustain, are about rolling out the improvement strategy, and then sustaining the benefits of the change through continuous improvement.

Change is cyclical, and so AGM is a cycle.

One change sets the context for the next change, the next step up.

You might be of a similar mindset to former Intel boss Andy Grove in that "only the paranoid survive." Perhaps what drives you to grow is adrenaline and the pursuit of excellence. You might find the idea of change being constant motivates you to be your best.

You might also be of the mindset that you'll "work hard now so I don't have to work as hard later!" You'll plant the seeds now so you can go on to enjoy the fruits of your labor. You want to create a particular kind of life and a legacy. In our method, the cycle of change shouldn't become an endless treadmill, rather a mechanism to move forward to the next stage.

As we alluded to earlier, there is often a tipping point in organizational transformation where things simply start to work better. You've gained momentum the same way you would by starting a heavy wheel spinning. You've pushed the accelerator, now it takes less energy to keep the car in motion. Although there will always be more to do, where you go next is up to you.

Since this book is about a leadership journey, as we close out the introduction, let's bring this back to a personal perspective.

Sir John Whitmore, father of the personal coaching industry, is known for the GROW model. GROW stands for future *Goal*, current *Reality*, possible *Options* to bridge the gap between current reality and future goal, and finally what you *Will* do to move forward.

Take a moment to visualize what you'll do, think, and become after putting the ideas in this book into practice. Finally, imagine what will happen if you *do not* step up. How will you feel? What will you miss out on? How will those surrounding you at work and at home be affected?

GROW is an example of a *gap-closure* approach to improvement. The gap in gap-closure is the difference between where you are today and where you want to be in the future.

Gap-closure approaches are also very commonly used in organizational change and transformation, and customer and market transformation.

AGM, which you just heard about, is an example of a gap-closure approach to organizational change. Once again, we see that personal growth and organizational growth overlap. The principles and practices are similar, and specifically in the case of Ascending/GX it is the alchemy of organizational, customer/market, and people growth that creates the magic.

Starting with a detailed future goal lets us see the current situation and road ahead more clearly, which makes it easier to spot new opportunities and solutions. Without a future orientation we get stuck playing *whack-a-mole* with current issues instead of exploring what the rest of the carnival has to offer.

AGM, like personal coaching, also builds *accountability* into each stage of the project and strategy. We build mutual accountability across the organization around doing what needs to be done to win together.

To bring the content to life, we recommend using GROW to make quick notes on where you are now, where you should be, and how to close the gap. You can use GROW to structure boardrooms and customer presentations, so it is one to add to your personal and professional toolkit in addition to AGM.

For now, let's return to you and personal growth. Stop and take a moment to write down your answers to the following questions:

1. Organizational Goals – What do you hope that this book will help you to deliver in the context of the organization?

2. Professional Goals – What do you hope to achieve after reading this book in terms of goals for the Marketing function and your career?

3. Personal Goals – How do you hope to grow as the result of reading this book?

Finally, let's consider how to get the most out of this book.

The Structure of this Book and How to Use it

This book is split into two parts. Part One comprises ten chapters that cover each of the elements of the Revenue Generation Value Chain in detail. We explain what each component is, how it fits into the whole, and share leading practices and implementation lessons for each area.

Part Two details the AGM approach to change, including practical advice and a case study for making the ideas in Part One a reality.

To get the most out of Part One, we recommend that you make notes on the current issues and opportunities in your organization that relate to what you're reading in each chapter.

It is best to think of specific scenarios and then try to determine the impact of possible issues. For example, perhaps you've lost several new customer acquisition pitches because the organization didn't have the right people in the room or wasn't able to put your solution in the context of the customer's business.

If you are extra diligent, you can assign each of the 10 areas in Part One a score from 1 (low maturity) to 10 (high maturity) or use traffic lights: red (high impact problems), amber (minor issues), or green (working well) based on your current knowledge of your organization. The example spiderweb diagram below provides a holistic glance on where a company is at in terms of its revenue generation maturity level for each practice area. The bigger and rounder the web is the higher maturity its practices are and therefore the more capable it is in achieving or exceeding its revenue goals.

Illustration 5: Revenue Generation Maturity Assessment

Assigning a rating is simply another trick to help you engage with the material and get the full value from it. You'll be starting to build a case for change and potential focus areas for further data gathering in the Data stage of AGM.

Throughout the book, we'll refer to *Marketing* (capitalized) to refer to the Marketing function or team, and lower-case *marketing* to refer to marketing process and activities (and the same with Sales and Customer to refer to those functions respectively).

While this book is focused on revenue growth through new business acquisition, we recognize the ongoing importance of brand in the complete picture of marketing and revenue. Instead of trying to duplicate some of the great resources available on brand marketing, in this book we'll take the approach of highlighting the key links between demand generation and brand. We hope that for brand marketers this book remains a readable and pragmatic primer that will help build out the complete picture of technology enabled B2B marketing in the current age.

Part Two is made up of five chapters that detail the AGM approach (Align, Data, Design, Deploy, and Sustain) to implementing a new strategy or transformational project.

We'll talk about the importance of vision and the case for change in Part Two, and that comes from developing an overall, and a granular "story" of the problems and opportunities within your organization. The notes you make in Part One are "real work" in developing and refining that story of change, so don't skip recording your notes.

There are no prizes for racing through this book. Take the time to understand the models and how they apply to your organization.

To complete the Revenue Generation Maturity Assessment online for your organization, go to https://www.the-growth-engine.com/

We are building a community of Ascending Marketers around the ideas in this book, please connect with us on LinkedIn at *Ascending Marketers.*

Remember the birds at the start of this chapter? Perhaps what we're really selling in this book above all is personal freedom. You grow so that you can have increased self-determination, and more regularly experience that feeling of soaring in your work and life.

It is time to get started.

It is time to take the next step.

It is time to ascend.

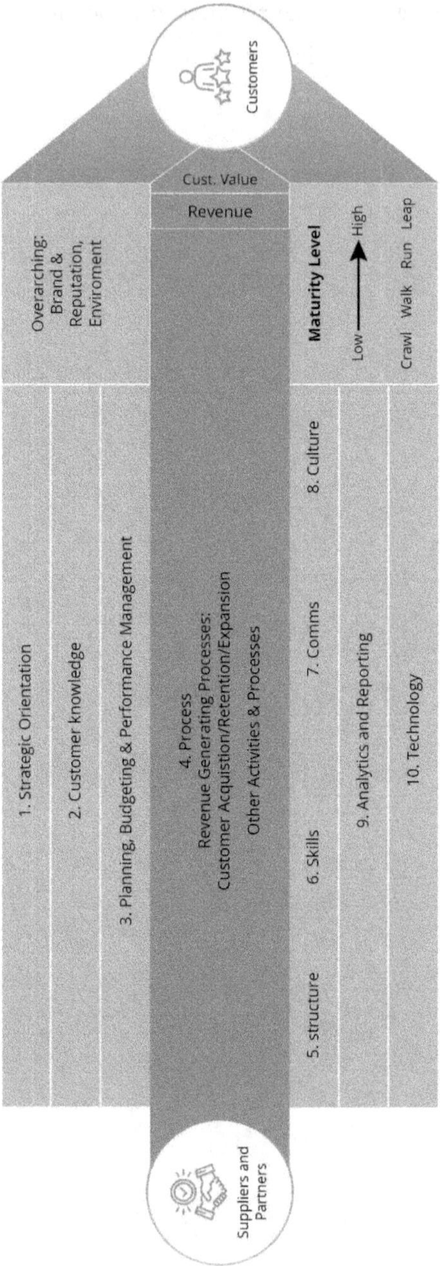

ASCENDING GROWTH

Customers

Cust. Value

Revenue

Overarching: Brand & Reputation, Enviroment

Maturity Level

Low → High

Crawl   Walk   Run   Leap

1. Strategic Orientation

2. Customer knowledge

3. Planning, Budgeting & Performance Management

4. Process
Revenue Generating Processes:
Customer Acquistion/Retention/Expansion

Other Activities & Processes

5. structure

6. Skills

7. Comms

8. Culture

9. Analytics and Reporting

10. Technology

Suppliers and Partners

Building the Growth Engine using GX

In Part One, we'll take a deep dive into each of the 10 components of the Revenue Generation Value Chain (RVC). The purpose of Part One is to give you a solid grounding in the 10 components and to illustrate how the RVC works hand-in-hand with Growth Experience (GX). Armed with this knowledge, you can perform an audit of your organization's current processes and build a blueprint for the future.

Each chapter includes a description of what low performing practices across the 10 areas typically look like to help guide your audit. We call these "descending" practices. There is also a description of "ascending" practices, which represent better or leading practices.

Then, you'll be able to use the Ascending Growth Method (AGM), which we'll describe in detail in Part Two. You'll learn to define a transformation program, close gaps between today and the future, and unlock the benefits of growth.

As you go through Part One reflect on how what you are hearing relates to your organization.

Let's get started!

Get ready for the onramp to empowerment, freedom, and joy! Invest the time to master the information in this book, and you'll develop a powerful new perspective supported by practical frameworks, which will allow you to take control of where you go next!

1

Strategic Orientation

Brett: *"Maalaea Bay, Maui lies eight thousand one hundred and ninety-eight kilometers northeast of Sydney, Australia. The morning sun is shining, and the passengers are shuffling about the boat with a mixture of tiredness and nervous energy as we steam across the bay to the Molokini Island Preserve. Despite the pleasant environment, I have several pressing business issues tempering my mood. My family has gone up to the front of the boat and I am alone at the back, staring at the white bubbly wake. A founder, a lone leader, staring at the infinite ocean and wondering what to do next.*

My business has lacked clear direction and good vibes in recent times, unlike the boat I now stood on. I was doing too many disparate things, fighting through quicksand, and not getting around to the projects I really wanted to do with others.

Suddenly I saw movement in the corner of my vision. Little silver darts, flying fish, defying gravity, and then plunging back into the water to repeat the joyous cycle.

I took a deep breath and thought back to my first business. The almost comical lack of strategy and planning that surrounded it. But I also remembered the abundant focus on the main event, teamwork and…love. The 'fish' jumped in the boat back in those days. We all worked tirelessly to build something great together. The business wasn't started for the money, but the money piled up, one creased ten-dollar bill at a time, then by the thousands.

When did I get so paralyzed by choices and fear and let the grind replace the grin?

What is strategy for if not to save you from too many options and counter-productive efforts? A weight suddenly lifted, my eyes moving forward with the path of the fish, ocean spray wisping. Keep it simple, focus on the one thing. Follow the love. Serendipity seems to show up but only when you have a direction. The show put on by the flying fish continued and I realized that I was smiling.

Do less to achieve more."

In this chapter we'll be using the word *strategic* in two ways. We will use the literal sense of "to do with the organizational strategy and planning process." In addition to that, we will use it to mean having the characteristics or traits of being "visionary, customer/market aware, holistic, focused", and so on. Specifically, we'll be talking about how to use strategic thinking to see new possibilities and stimulate growth, and to align the organization to those activities that both drive the economic engine *and* delight new and existing customers.

At the most basic level, strategic orientation involves aligning marketing activity to the overall business objectives and go-to-market approach. In more advanced forms, strategic orientation enabled by the Marketing team, becomes, or at least helps shape the overall business direction.

Now let's look at *Strategic Orientation* in the context of organizational practices and growth.

1. Organizational Growth

Strategic Orientation in the Revenue Generation Value Chain model is defined as the degree to which a firm is future focused. It sets a positive direction towards growth and seeks to align the parts of the organization to deliver on that growth.

To what degree is your organization future-focused now? Is it looking forward (beyond the next quarter) or stuck looking in the rear-view mirror? If it is seeking growth, are there any substantive insights or ideas supporting how the growth number will be achieved?

If your organizational practices are "descending" at the moment, or you suspect that they are, this indicates the need to do a more detailed review of the current situation in that area, and to look for opportunities to improve.

The descending practices we'll describe are all based on real examples, and you might feel an uncomfortable sense of recognition in some of them. As with a fish not being able to see the water, we can't always see or articulate what needs to be changed in a specific situation.

The purpose of the descending and ascending statements is to give you a sense of what to look for when you perform an audit of your current business. Of course, these do not represent every potential situation or opportunity but do serve as a useful and practical guide.

Let's start by looking at a set of practices that are *not* usually associated with the ability to *sustainably* grow.

Descending ("vicious cycle")

Firms with low strategic orientation often lack strategic direction beyond the need to "sell more product."

These firms might be successful and even show some growth. Perhaps the firm is enjoying a first-mover market advantage or is a new startup expanding quickly because of the strength of its founders and a solid product/market fit.

An organization might have grown by being opportunistic in acquisitions or buying market share, while simultaneously diluting focus and acquiring a long tail of products and unprofitable customers.

Of course, the organization might simply have hit the wall in terms of running out of new ideas, or new tactics to respond to competitors. Revenue might be plateauing or plummeting.

Firms at this stage of maturity are often highly reactive. This feels like being a passenger on a ship in rough seas even when the weather is calm. Various departments appear to be heading in different directions and often with goals at odds with each other. At the same time these departments rarely communicate except to assign blame for missed targets.

Marketing is often sidelined in descending organizations, waiting for the next budget cut after a soft quarter of sales. The primary measure of

Marketing is activity-based, rather than outcome-based. The firm has little identity outside of the products and services it sells, and those product and service portfolios seem to have little rhyme or reason in how they've been put together, or how they are linked with planned synergies.

In these companies, the vision, mission, and purpose are generic because of the low effort expended on creating them. They appear on the website but are almost never used to motivate and engage anyone inside or outside of the organization.

Next let's look at practices that typically set the organization on the path to growth.

Ascending ("virtuous cycle")

Firms with higher strategic orientation have a formal strategy development process and/or a unifying idea of what the firm represents for its customers and how to execute on that.

The strategy is used throughout the organization and updated regularly. It is the norm for Marketing and other functions to integrate the overall strategy when developing their own plans. Needless "off strategy" directions or initiatives are rare and either stopped by the governance process or quickly reigned in, including through "peer pressure" from the leadership team. The strategy and vision are simply the drumbeat to which the organization works.

The strategy development process incorporates both external and internal analysis and what-if scenarios looking several years into the future. An evaluation of risks and potential disruptions is done to evaluate risk within the strategy. Those risks are monitored for triggering events, and processes are in place for what to do should strategic risks translate to issues.

Work has been performed, based on real data, to refine both the product/service, and business portfolio to focus on core strategic elements and differentiating strengths.

Customer/market segments have been created and refined using real data, and there is a data-based view of market profitability to support strategic decision making on where to focus, and importantly, where not to focus. The business model is clear down to the level of revenue generating processes, and the operating model aligns with this.

A clear view exists of "who we are" as a business connecting brand, product, and services to customers, employees, and company culture. A good strategy helps move both the hearts and the minds of employees, partners, and customers.

At the same time, the organization continuously looks outwards to customers and partners to find new opportunities that add value.

Needless to say, firms in this group are well on track with customer experience (CX) and have digital transformation as a strategic focus.

Above all of this, these firms seem to really know and love their customers. They are passionate about their products and services and helping the customer grow in their business. Listening to customers might seem like olde-timey business advice, yet it is still a great strategy because, so few firms do it well. Knowing your customer also allows you to offer them what they *don't* yet know that they need, and that lets you stay one step ahead.

As your focus on numbers and analytics increases, don't lose "heart." It's the heart that differentiates you (and the firm) from everyone else that does the same.

In Practice

The first step in developing strategic orientation is to ensure that Marketing's house is in order by developing a quality Marketing Strategy, *especially* when you don't have time to do so, or you feel that there are many things outside your control!

A strategy is more than simply the sum of your planned demand generation and brand building activities. It gets to the core of how to use customer and market insights to decide where to focus to create value and drive growth.

The value of the marketing strategy comes as much from *how* you develop it as the final document. You'll meet with your peers in other functions, including Sales and Finance, to talk through your thoughts and to get feedback, which is important for alignment and interlock.

By meeting with different parts of the organization, you gain a dynamic perspective and fill in "blind spots" in your knowledge of the firm. As a result, you'll build a more comprehensive and complete picture of where growth opportunities might be.

At the basic level you'll start creating your strategy by developing a solid point of view on the market (industries, sectors, and market specifics) and trends, customer, and competitor insights.

You'll consider things like pre-existing strategy and market documentation, conversations with others inside and outside the firm, and potentially input from third party agencies or consultancies. Use any of the tools at your disposal to analyze this data, which could even include the PESTEL and SWOT techniques you learnt in first year marketing class.

Observe how competitors go to market, and then take a critical look at your own company's presence. Find any major areas of misalignment or opportunities. Is your company expecting to grow yet the market is shrinking or evolving, and the marketing budget is almost non-existent? What sort of data and statistics can you get to support your ideas and conclusions?

This baseline of information can inform further detailed conversations with different parts of the organization, and will help build the case for "what needs to be different?" as well as "why change?"

Develop a clear view of what the go-to-market (GTM) strategy is for the business or specific business unit, and in case of a regional operation, understand how this strategy translates for different markets.

All too often, we find that the GTM is not clearly articulated at each level of the organization whether globally or regionally. This doesn't mean you should ignore GTM, instead seek to clarify how Marketing will support the GTM strategy and work with other teams effectively.

It's also important to have clearly articulated Sales "plays," so that Marketing can tailor its strategy to support those. For example, an organization might successfully enter a market with a particular sales approach but if they don't evolve as the market matures, they might be stuck with an outdated approach, be a "one trick pony," or in an overly narrow niche. By working with Sales, you'll enhance these plays to move the customer through the orbit of Acquisition, Expansion, and Retention.

The firm might articulate a desire for growth, but not put in effort to align Marketing, Sales, and Customer Success with the GTM. You must understand how different parts of the firm need to align to chase down growth.

Your strategy and associated plan will also need to contain clear objectives, goals, and KPIs. This is often easier said than done as organizations at the Walk/Crawl stage, low maturity in core capabilities of RVC, are not effective at translating growth targets into meaningful objectives across teams. It's hard for Marketing to be effective and effectively develop strategy if the overall organizational targets and goals are not clearly set.

Lastly, a third key alignment point centers around customer insights and understanding of the Ideal Customer Profile (ICP), drivers and the play-to-win strategy. We'll continue that discussion in the next chapter.

"In a number of roles, I encountered a similar situation - whether it was a well-established enterprise organization that was a market leader and growth was stalling or it was a startup/SMB in a high growth market, but the business and marketing teams were not achieving set targets.

In one organization (global information and technology company) that I joined as a Solution and Segment Marketing Manager, the company launched a new product offer to the banking and financial services industry but found that they were not getting the market penetration and projected sales.

Business was stagnant after two years in the market. As a newly appointed marketing manager for this segment and product line, I took a zero-based strategy and planning approach to understand the root causes and why we were failing. This led me to the original business case that was developed several years prior, which did not take into consideration the changing market dynamic and customer needs.

Some of the factors that shifted the market were regulation and an aggressive competitor that entered the market before our product was launched. These insights (among others) supported the review and revamping of the overall go-to-market strategy and introduction of a two-prong strategy that gave way to specific sales and marketing plays.

Play one: enterprise, niche and high value solution play, part of a long-term approach to flank and displace a well-entrenched competitor; and Play 2: transactional sales play with broader market appeal that could immediately bring in revenue. This was supported by a brand-to-demand type of marketing strategy, resulting in a $2M pipeline in the first three months.

Fast forward five years and today this division is the #1 revenue driver for this global technology organization. The example here depicts a clear need to revisit the strategy often and never be afraid to challenge the status quo!" - Ljubica Radoicic

2. Customer/Market

Adopting GX as the core of your strategy, as well as focusing on techniques such as Account Based Marketing (ABM), will begin to affect how you might think about go-to-market and what success looks like from a customer/market perspective. Taking a customer centric approach instead of "spray and pray," you'll be using actual data identifying specific potential customers to focus and tailor your approach to both Sales and Marketing.

Moving from product selling to solution selling makes sense because customers have always cared more about their own problems than they do about your products! Yet B2B firms, often emerging from a technical and product-centric culture, feel most comfortable talking about themselves.

The challenge with focusing on products is that innovation inevitably slows down as markets mature, and it becomes harder for the customer to differentiate based on product specs alone.

Moving to solution selling is a step forward in recognizing that the overall brand experience is as important as the core product.

Having customers interested in an overall experience rather than product features influences how you craft and execute a differentiation strategy.

This might include returning to the big questions of "what is our real value as a company?", "how do we define the market we operate in" and "why do customers buy?" If this sounds complicated or abstract, it needn't be.

For example, helping your customer win might be as simple as offering enhanced reporting, forecasting, or billing to minimize low or no value activities.

In B2B, further insights will come from considering what is important to your *customer's* customers. How can your product or service help solve problems further down the chain that help your client win?

Marketing will need to play a key role in helping the organization know who their existing and potential customers are, both by type (i.e., segments, personas) and individually (i.e., tracked in CRM, or looking up website visitors). Improving strategic orientation means ensuring that customer and market insight are fed back into the strategy setting process.

Suggestions from customers or solutions developed with the customer can become a significant differentiator, and even a source of competitive advantage. The ability to listen and act can become strategic itself, particularly when the market is in a period of rapid change.

Of course, becoming strategically oriented doesn't only mean listening to customers or looking externally for insights once. It means having the processes, people, and structures to turn this strategic listening into a repeatable *capability.*

Many firms have or are considering adding a Chief Revenue Officer (CRO) role to boost revenue. Having a CRO is not a strategy in itself! Without proper guidance, the CRO role might veer off into areas that are not only not strategic but also not profitable either.

The *Three Horizons* idea from Baghani, Coley, and White's *The Alchemy of Growth* might be a useful addition from a strategic perspective. In short, the three horizons are a strategic growth pipeline for businesses.

Horizon 1 focuses on extending and defending existing core businesses. Horizon 2 is about building emerging businesses. Horizon 3 is focused on creating viable options for the future. Each horizon has different measures and requirements from marketing. For example, Horizon 2 focuses on scaling and optimizing the business model (rather than only on profit). Strategy is about making choices, including on where to place bets now and in the future.

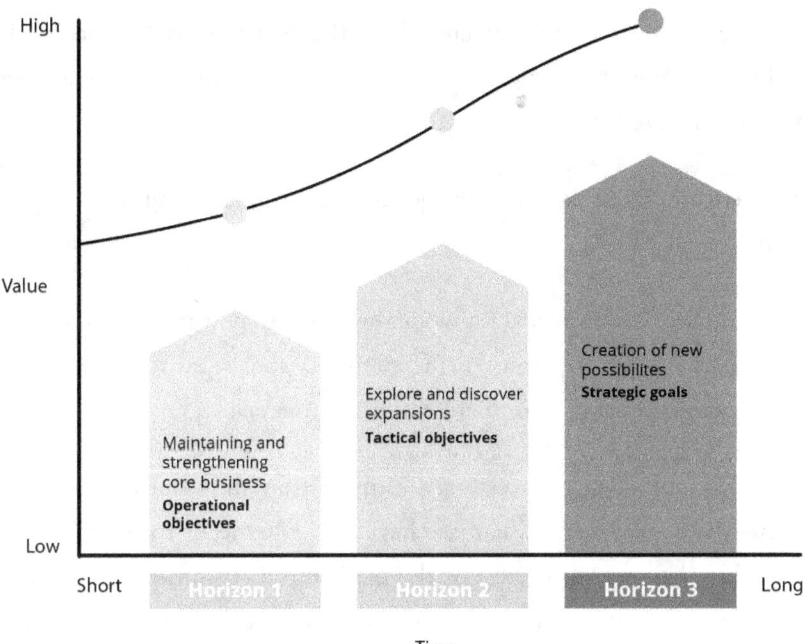

Illustration 6: Three Horizons

3. People

The transformation of Marketing and the rest of the organization is also a professional and personal transformation of *you*.

It sounds obvious, but the starting point for being more strategic is to take time to work *on* the business rather than *in* it. This means taking a step back from day-to-day activities, to look at the big picture and how Marketing and you can support the organization to reach its goals.

Starting with the end in mind, this professional transformation process is you becoming a well-rounded, trusted business leader. It is not enough to only be great at marketing. A strategic Marketing leader feels comfortable in the commercial engine of the business, is familiar with technology and takes a holistic perspective of the business as it is now and could be in future.

Your overall goal might be a bigger marketing role, or onwards to becoming a CEO.

The reality of where you are now might be far away from that! The first steps are to build on your existing strengths and begin to work across the organization and in an increasingly commercial way.

As we've said already, investing the time in building out a marketing strategy is a good start. What you have, and what leads to your "seat at the table" is your knowledge of the market and customer. In the next chapter we'll talk about the practices and processes of developing and using Customer Knowledge.

It's also important to get more comfortable with always having KPIs, facts, and numbers to support your strategies when interacting with team members outside of Marketing.

Often, you'll need to be the cheerleader, evangelist, or ambassador for Marketing within the broader organization, or some combination of all three. If Marketing has been sidelined, then you'll need to tell people what the real value of Marketing to the organization and to *them* is. This might not feel comfortable, but this is where courage and the leadership to bring your team along comes in.

Being more strategic might translate to shielding your team from constant changes and reactivity coming from outside Marketing. By having the process discipline to align with leaders outside of Marketing, you set your team up for success, and can help the team see how their work connects with the big picture. The team will also have the opportunity to step up and take increased ownership of their work, both inside and outside of Marketing.

For now, what are the 2-3 things that you can apply from this chapter to be more strategic in your approach? What is the simplest thing that you can put into practice that would make a meaningful difference to the strategic orientation of Marketing/the organization?

We suggest you start with the following actions:

- Define and communicate a purpose and destination for your department.
- Build and nurture a team culture of trust and leadership. Learn from your team.
- Align your personal and organizational focus, then do the same for your individual team members. They need to own it after all.
- Balance long term vision with short term goals and maintain an agile approach. Take time to reflect the actions in short- and long-term perspectives.
- Check your rhetoric - are you speaking the language of business/revenue or are you stuck in "marketing speak?"

Key Takeaways:

- Being strategic includes being forward looking and incorporating both internal (organizational) and external (customer/market) perspectives.

- Although Marketing is well placed to be the oracle for customer and market knowledge, it must first get its own house in order by building a collaborative strategy with other departments.

- GX is a strategic lever focusing on helping customers win.

- Strategic Orientation provides executives with a new way of examining their business. It allows them to create new capabilities and improve existing operations.

- Strategic Orientation paves the way for organizations to become innovative, achieving a competitive advantage and long-term growth. It determines whether a company will "thrive" rather than only surviving.

2

Customer Knowledge

"Know yourself. Know your business. Know your customer. Know your customer's business."

Marsha Clark, Authentic leadership,
and executive development coach

Since it sits at the core of any successful business, organizations should excel at gathering and using customer knowledge to gain competitive advantage. Customer knowledge is about understanding needs, goals, wants, and emotional reasons for buying. This knowledge helps firms focus on their customers' most valuable needs, which ultimately increases the perceived value and switching costs of a firm's products.

Customer knowledge can assist employees with cross-selling as well as efficiently predicting market demand, which helps to leverage competitive advantage more effectively. Without this knowledge, it would be impossible for a company to provide first class customer service, ensure customized products and services, and align its business processes and operations so that it is able to forge strong relationships.

You'd be hard pressed to find an organization that doesn't say that they are "customer first" at least in principle. Despite this, our research shows that only 22% of organizations know their customers well.

According to a 2019 McKinsey survey, 65% of businesses say the customer insights function should be a "thought partner" of the entire organization. The *2020 Revenue Generation Maturity Study* found that of the 66% who believe they have better practice in this area, 85% of them achieved their revenue goals in the previous 12 months. On the contrary, those who rated themselves poorly in 'Knowing your customers' only 1.5% achieved their revenue goals in the previous 12 months.

GX raises the bar on customer interactions. It not only helps you know the customer in greater detail, but also helps change up the customer conversation. It can even change our own *thinking* about what the ultimate value of the customer is (and what it might be).

What if the customer conversation was a two-way street?

Technology that allows us to know customers purely from their data comes at the risk that we'll sacrifice our real connection with them, and that each of us will be worse off as a result.

1. Organizational Growth

Again, let's start by looking at low maturity practices with customer knowledge. Do you see any of these in play out in your current organization?

Descending

Companies in this group have little detailed knowledge about their prospective or even their existing customers, and the approach to customers is largely reactive and transactional.

There is a general sense of who the customer is because of the sales process and product, but this knowledge doesn't extend to specific pain points or drivers. Where segments exist, they tend to be based only on firmographic data and sales territories and rarely updated.

Marketing materials tend to be generic and talk mainly about the features of the product or service and the organization itself. There is very little, if any, thought given to the buyer's journey, personas, or differences between segments. Many of the marketing materials produced are never used.

At the same time, it is difficult to get reliable customer data since there is no single view of the customer due to little integration between CRM, ERP, and MAS. In fact, there are often competing versions of the truth between departments like Marketing, Sales, and Finance.

Poor customer knowledge leads to poor targeting. For example, perhaps the Sales team is targeting a hands-on user rather than targeting a higher-level leader at the prospective organization who has a more strategic view, larger scope, and a bigger budget. Because of this the product could be viewed as a commodity since differentiation and value were not articulated to the right buyer. The result might be low value deals, and a failure to scale initial sales into ongoing "strategic" accounts that deliver revenue over an extended period.

Ascending

Companies in this group have developed detailed ideal customer profiles, which are shared across the organization.

Persona profiles are defined clearly for each solution/product line with demographic, psychographic, and behavioral data for each persona. Buyer journey maps are clearly defined for each persona too. Multiple personas are developed to cover all the major buying roles.

There is often a taskforce formed to review these datasets on a periodical basis (every 6 or 12 months) to ensure they are up to date. Continuous improvement processes have been put in place to allow sharing of customer knowledge across the organization.

Systems are fully integrated, between CRM, MAS, ERP, and the tools used by customer service to provide a 360-degree view of the customer. Offline customer interactions are documented and shared as well, not just digital activities. There is a Voice of the Customer Program (VOC) in place and prioritization structure has been defined. There are clear KPIs, and performance management measures put in place to ensure data integrity and knowledge sharing. Customer line of sight goals have been set at team and individual levels.

In Account Based Marketing (ABM), or customer marketing initiatives, it's a shared effort between departments. A customer task force is formed with members from different departments which share account intelligence and current challenges, and necessary actions are taken by relevant team members to resolve those challenges.

Meaningful personalization is in place using ABM and other customer marketing data to create a unique experience for the buyer.

Products, services, or solutions for companies in this group show clear market positioning and add value at both *Brand* and *Product/Solution* levels to solve strategic customer challenges.

In Practice

The recent pandemic has accelerated digital use in the B2B space and left companies scrambling to ensure that digital and social channels not only *work* to meet increasing customer expectations, but also that firms can take advantage of the array of new customer data available.

To examine that more, let's look at Segmentation, Personas, and Journey Maps as ways to build and use customer knowledge in Marketing and across the organization.

Segmentation

Segmentation is the foundation of an effective go-to-market (GTM) strategy and goes to the core of "how do we define our markets; where do we play and how do we win?" While the idea of segmentation is well established, the practice of segmentation is less uniform.

Firstly, in practice, the segments used by various departments often do not align.

For example, the segments used by the Sales team might be based on territory, industry or organization size or even an "other" bucket (e.g., one containing both SMEs and multi-million dollar companies that don't fit into other groups).

At the same time, segments used by Marketing could be based on behavior of the primary buyer and other psychographic information.

Because of this discrepancy with Sales, the goal posts keep moving in terms of key segments. If there is a lack of communication, Sales and Marketing may not both be aligned with the most profitable segments, which affects growth.

The Sales team may even be structured differently in each country or state, making it hard for marketing to align and support them. In global companies operating across regions there can be a lack of local GTM strategy, so Sales are left to come up with a strategy, segment markets and define where they play.

Secondly, the ability to create high-value segments is often inhibited by the quality and availability of data across the company data stores. Related to this, the segments may have been created a while ago, and now be out of date. Just because previously defined segments exist it doesn't mean that they are current or useful.

One reason for low quality outcomes from segmentation is that there may not be a consistent and data-driven methodology for segmentation in place. There can be the case where segments represent a particular person or group's *opinion* on where the organization should focus, rather than analysis of value. This can mean that segmentation becomes political instead of analytical when it comes to updating these segments. You should be ready to help make the case for fact-based segmentation.

In practice, your job will be to begin using this data-based approach to segments, proving their value, and to align these new segments with the Sales team.

Unfortunately, the reality is that even if businesses do generally know who their customers are, they still prefer to talk about themselves. All their campaigns, content, and materials are product centric! This is a matter to be picked up at various levels of your new strategy for change and might be called "customer centricity" as an umbrella term. Knowledge isn't power until you use that knowledge to create value for the business (and the customer).

Personas

We all recognize the importance of Personas (characters created to represent buyer types) to tailor marketing efforts. In B2B marketing, it's also critical to be able to think in terms of multiple personas and to identify these personas' main role in the process. For example: decision maker, influencer, champion, end user, blocker/gate keeper, and so on.

It's not just enough to create personas, they (like segments) also have to be used consistently across the organization. For example, at a regional firm, personas were introduced in Marketing and their communication with the customer became more sophisticated and targeted. So far, so good. However, Sales were still lagging. Personas (buying committee roles) were not reflected in the CRM, so these roles were not effectively targeted, so any traction Marketing created was lost.

As with segments, personas will be refined by Marketing and Sales working together, with Marketing effectively articulating the value of the improved targeting that personas provide. Improved personas/targeting should result in improved win rates, and larger deal sizes.

When I was the head of marketing for a global output technology solution provider, the company experienced a 97% customer retention rate. One of the major factors of the company's success was a clear understanding of ideal customers as well as the key personas along the customer experience journey. The company took a value journey approach to help enterprise clients optimize their practice. For example, customers signed up for a five-year Managed Print Services (MPS) contract and then used the company's "Print Less Save More" methodology to optimize their information throughput and output. This is instrumental in achieving "customer for life" goals. This approach also helped the company to continuously evolve to acquire or develop solutions that solve their customer's ongoing and future challenges.

While customers printed less based on the company's MPS (Managed Print Services) strategies, the firm acquired a dozen workflow software companies and was successful in adding continuous value to its customers. As a result, this generated ongoing revenue growth within those accounts. - Eve Chen

Journey Maps

While they are called *customer* journey maps, you'll often need to do one for each *persona*. It is critical that you have up to date quality personas to put into the journey map process. The maps are often created based on generic buying stages, but you can also use the ones your organization uses or refine the standard ones by talking with your customers.

You might find that stages need to be split, or new ones added (sparingly) to tell the whole story.

You might create the journey maps in Marketing to understand touchpoints with the brand across buying stages. They might be produced as part of a CX initiative, or you might do them as a cross-functional performance improvement effort. While considering the ideal journey, you'll also document issues and "red flags" with the current process. As you think about the future, you'll not only want to fix today's problems, but also level-up and go beyond your competitors to delight the customer.

Account Knowledge

The next layer of knowledge is account knowledge e.g., through ABM or a business development-based account management process.

Depending on your organization's current level of Sales and Marketing alignment and overall technical sophistication, we often recommend conducting an ABM pilot with a small number of key accounts or even a single account to build learnings and shared goals between teams.

The process of running a pilot allows success factors to be discovered and documented. It also allows the roles and responsibilities to become clearer, aligns goals, and clarifies processes that allow members in the pilot project to work as a team on customer journey. You'll also need to have a plan and process for how this pilot project is developed and expanded.

In practice there is always a need to pilot, test, and refine segmentation, personas, journey maps, and account tailoring.

An information management solution provider in the large capital construction industry engaged my team to design and develop a One to Few ABM program. 30 days into the project it became very clear that the client was not ready for such an undertaking.

Using a methodical approach to develop an ABM program was critical. The best practice approach required us to start with the alignment of the internal teams around goals, expected outcomes, and working together to select the right accounts to target for the program before the Design phase can take place.

Without a clear picture of their ideal customer profile and persona profiles, journey maps could not be developed. At the same time, this company was going through massive internal restructuring and as a result Sales teams were not allocated their new accounts and segments to target. The exercise of putting together an ABM program clearly crystalized a few internal struggles to create an effective program to target their strategic accounts.

The end result saw us turning this ABM program into a more generic demand generation program, but it highlighted invaluable lessons and challenges the management team had to address to ensure their teams were ready for such transition into a more focused targeting program. - Eve Chen

2. Customer/Market

"Your customers don't care about you, your products, or your services. They care about themselves, their wants, and their needs." - Joe Pulizzi, Author

We know that B2B customers increasingly view *overall* customer experience as being equally important to quality and price when making a purchasing decision. The response to this has been CX on the organizational side; an attempt to differentiate from, or match, competitive industry service levels and reduce friction in the buyer's transaction.

This includes managing omnichannel touchpoints with the company. According to Salesforce.com, the average consumer is now using 10 channels to communicate with businesses. This diverse array of channels raises the bar on customer journey complexity with 80% of customers now considering their experience with a company to be as important as its products.

As we've said several times, CX has helped B2B firms level up service, respond to the pandemic, and become as smooth as Teflon. Despite the effort to remove friction, we see a countertrend in B2C customers embracing friction by lining up for new restaurants, smartphones, and limited-edition clothing and footwear. This additional effort and time spent somehow enhances the overall experience with, and loyalty to the brand.

Perhaps there is a risk of over-focusing on analytics and seamlessness at the expense of finding opportunities to wow the customer and build lifelong relationships? You have to at least ask yourself this question!

A notable development in looking at the buyer is to use the concept of the Hero's Journey to place the buyer in a story. While storytelling in branding is commonplace, a principle of story *branding* is to position the customer as the hero rather than the brand itself. The entire interaction is framed as a story, helping the customer overcome a major challenge to become successful. Instead of saying "we're great," the firm says, "we're here to make you great."

Now, what next?

The next step is to broadly consider the question: "what is success?" for the buyer and customer firm. And the answer will affect the way you segment, develop personas, and outline the customer journey.

For example, is the value *to* the customer only related to product features and price? No. So what is the value to them? And what other value could we deliver to the customer?

Is the value *of* the customer to the business only the immediate sales made? What about lifetime value vs. initial transaction? What about referrals and recommendations? The customer providing you strategic insight and ideas about the market, and your products and services? What about co-development of innovation? What value and possibilities would come from partnering with customers for growth?

We argue that success for buyers and customers is ultimately growth in one form or another, whether expressed in terms of profitable growth, career growth, growth in meaning and contribution. The challenge under GX is finding the win-win-win at the overlap of Organizational, Customer, and People value.

B2B buyers are looking for more than minimizing "total cost of ownership" or improved delivery times. They not only want to feel part of something bigger, but they also want to see the positive impact of dealing with you reflected in the progression of their goals.

One way to get at this with GX is to develop psychographic and multiple buyer personas to better answer the question of "what does growth look like for our customers?" It also helps to ask *them* open-ended questions like this to change up the conversation.

In GX, it is particularly important to understand customer business goals and growth targets as well as challenges they face to meet those targets. In other words, we need to understand each key persona's responsibilities in achieving revenue goals and how the buying process works in their organization.

With the evolution of B2B marketing and personalization via technology enabled Account Based Marketing (ABM), we can envisage that each of the selling firm's focus accounts will have an increasingly tailored support structure in place from the firm to support those focus customers to succeed and grow.

With GX, it's important to look at value creation for customers across different elements of the value chain and to articulate how those drive better outcomes for the customer.

Understanding the potential value creation opportunities can be accomplished through a series of cross functional workshops that explore what optimization is needed to improve delivery of services and customer interactions.

The journey map should not end at Customer Acquisition if the goal is to keep a customer for life, but it also shouldn't be static. Instead, it should evolve, and change based on your customers' changing needs.

If this is the future, then the present is that businesses already have some quality data/customer knowledge related to growth but fail to use it effectively.

For example, we know several technology companies (e.g., SaaS) that already have a vast treasure chest of customer data, yet the Marketing teams are still focused on the product and product roadmap, rather than seeking insights from customer data or the customers themselves.

These firms do get some continuous feedback that is passed along to engineering, yet customer insights are rarely used to look at how the firm solves customer problems. While keeping the vision of GX in mind, remember to look for immediate opportunities to better use the data your firm already has.

Another example of how the future might lie under GX, is to look at professional services firms that are structured in a matrix between solution and industry, which often use an account management structure to build sustainable relationships and make customers into clients.

These firms often hire industry experts and "subject matter experts" to provide inside knowledge, connections, and expertise supporting both the Sales and Marketing process.

In these firms, there is a well-developed account management structure. It is not uncommon for professional services firms to develop custom solutions and offerings for a single client (but then, of course, to attempt to market these to other clients).

Sometimes a professional services firm will know the client "better than themselves," and this type of knowledge is valuable to the client and the ongoing relationship.

The firm will also be abreast of industry trends and even the specifics of what other competitor firms are doing. Industry and market knowledge changes up the conversation with clients to be more contextualized and specific and thus more valuable. As a result, you'll be more likely to be seen as a trusted partner, rather than just a salesperson.

Understanding the political landscape at a specific client before making a sale is often needed in B2B firms. We talk frequently about finding a "champion" within the organization, and really sharing with them a clear picture of the business value of adopting your solution. This can help smooth the way to a sale and eventually an ongoing relationship.

The benefits for that individual champion usually include far more than "efficiency" or cost effectiveness for their firm. A set of personal values, including recognition, being seen as an innovator, and possible future career progression may influence their decision.

How could your firm change up the conversation with customers?

What one or two things jump out to you right now as problems/opportunities for how you could interact more broadly with customers today or could interact differently in future?

3. People

"Every time I felt a little bit of doubt, all I had to do was talk to our customers, and that inherently gave me so much conviction along the way." - Katrina Lake. CEO Stitch Fix

There is power in talking with customers and clients. When you're dealing with transforming an organization, it can be vital to check on all the different opinions, facts, and strategies by going back to the source, the customer.

Customer insight is powerful for you as a marketer since you want to position yourself as the voice of the customer and the customer oracle within the organization.

Getting outside your normal headspace is also powerful because it helps you overcome the feeling of working in the dark and dealing with abstractions.

GX and market demands will require leaders to work increasingly across traditional functional boundaries. The journey for the Ascending

Marketer will be to use and build on the market and customer knowledge that they develop, and to bring others along in delivering new types of value to the customer.

This is easier said than done. How to segment and target the market, and deal with prospects/customers is at the core of how the Sales team and the business operate and may have operated for some time.

You'd be right to assume that a fair amount of diplomacy is required to make changes in this area. You'd also be right if you think that you may get pushback on even the most self-evident concepts of being customer centric.

Your tendency might be to try to shy away from the inevitable "creative conflict" required to get real alignment on go-to-market strategy and segments, but without stepping up to make these changes happen, Marketing will be forever stuck in reactive mode.

What are two to three ideas you've gotten from this chapter that you might want to test or apply at your firm?

Key Takeaways:

- Performing Segmentation, Personas and Journey Maps is not enough, these must also be aligned between functions, and used across the organization.
- As part of GX it is necessary to challenge conventional wisdom, both around what is value to the customer, and the understanding of the true and complete value of the customer to the firm.
- Take regular opportunities for you and your team to speak directly with customers.

3

Planning, Budgeting and Performance Management

*"Unless commitment is made, there are only
promises and hopes; but no plans."*

Peter F Drucker, Management Expert

*"We were in a conference room at a steel mill a couple of hours out of Sydney.
The room was a little worn around the edges, not one that often saw guests,
but today there were indeed guests on the way. The Sales and Marketing
teams and Finance had been invited into the inner sanctum of the Operations building for a new type of alignment meeting, which, if successful,
would transform the way the organization worked and deliver millions of
dollars in benefits.*

*I distinctly remember the muted anticipation as the participants filed into
the room. The sun streaming through the windows, moist shirt collars. The
continuous whir of the air conditioner reminded us of all that, being No-
vember; the Southern Hemisphere summer was just around the corner.
Today was the culmination of what we'd been working on since the spring.*

Once everyone was seated, the Head of Operations planning, who was a short time from retirement, rose to address the group. Thinking back now, I remember his demeanor being something like a father at a wedding, proud and slightly nervous. I was proud too in a way, recalling that this had been a completely different bunch of people just a few months earlier. They'd been suspicious of the new transparency we sought to turn around some negative result trends, and a bit reluctant to do what seemed like more work.

The meeting got underway with the discussion of various sales forecasts, major bids in play, new products, and various promotions that might be activated to boost sales. We heard about the future railway lines and fence posts that would crisscross the red outback regions of Australia if these bids came through.

Under the sponsorship of Finance and Leadership, Operations had been the champions of the new process, because their decisions, in anticipation of what Sales and Marketing might do, were long term and difficult to change. It seemed less of a cliché than usual to liken Operations and the organization to an oil tanker, when we were surrounded on the site by millions of tons of equipment, and multiple "Sydney Harbor Bridges worth" of steel.

As the meeting progressed, I saw the metaphorical light bulbs on all sides of the table. Like water running into a dry riverbed after a drought, turning on the flow of information quenched their thirst for insights and shared understanding. Suddenly the different functions represented in the room had the same information, formerly "secret" siloed information and assumptions that were not accustomed to crossing departmental boundaries. They could now make decisions on what they'd heard and discussed (and the minutes would keep everyone honest). The meeting began to wind up and I felt behaviors had already begun to shift positively, and somehow the people in that room had changed too." - Brett Cowell

A focused pursuit of growth can produce impressive top-line revenues. However, business and marketing executives recognize that they will encounter challenges such as siloed teams, redundant capabilities, and gradual mission and vision creep as the business evolves and demands team change. All these can impede the pursuit of sustainable growth and profitability. According to the McKinsey Transformation Change survey, just 26 percent of companies accomplish their performance objectives. This is why the activities of planning, budgeting and performance management represent the foundation of any successful game plan!

However, it's rare to find people in the business world that get genuinely excited by the notion of planning. We seem to prefer to be firefighting in the trenches, needing to unleash heroic efforts to make the numbers for the month / quarter / year. All too often, "Planning gets in the way of real work," is the incorrect, but prevalent belief.

Reactivity might be what some of us are used to, but we all know that war and chaos are probably not the metaphors that we want to live our whole careers by. Chaotic activity is no way to run a business looking for sustainable growth. Will you be the one to help wean the business off its addiction to reactivity?

In this chapter, we'll describe why planning is even *more* important in this era and how to align those plans and the business. We'll talk about how to get the budget and annual planning process aligned for growth. We will also consider how to align incentives and the performance management mechanism to support teaming and growth.

Lastly, we'll talk about execution and setting the organization up for success since, along with Strategic Orientation and Customer

Knowledge, Planning represents part of the all-important "game plan" that we'll use to grow.

Let us ask you a question: How do *you* plan for growth?

1. Organizational Growth

In this section, we'll look at organizational growth aspects of A) Planning, B) Budgeting, and C) Performance management. Although these topics are interrelated, we've separated them for the purposes of organizational discussion to provide additional granularity, however when we look at the Customer/Market and People aspects, we'll discuss the three aspects together.

It is also worth noting that while we'll talk about Marketing planning and budgeting, you can't really do that well in a silo! As you are reading through, bear in mind that planning, budgeting, and performance management requires close coordination at all levels in the organization.

Let's start with planning, and the "descending" or low maturity practices we typically find in companies that are not set up for success.

A. Planning

Descending

The entirety of planning in Sales and Marketing is essentially creating a budget with sales and expense targets. There is a lack of strategic planning and any business planning that is done is not done as a team effort.

Marketing and Sales plans are often created in isolation. Marketing doesn't know the numbers and targets of different Sales teams. Account plans are not done at all, and account structures are unclear.

Organizations at this stage are typically very product centric so any marketing activity (including plans if they exist) is to support sales efforts like events, collateral, advertising, or product pushing. There is often no clear alignment of GTM strategy due to disconnected teams and multiple, competing priorities, such as Product, Sales, Marketing and Customer Success. All have their own agendas and direction. No real interlock.

Ascending

Mature organizations recognize that not only is planning real work (it's about real sales, real results down the track) but that there is a specific *hierarchy* of plans. From strategic planning and GTM, to budgeting, to functional plans, down to daily pipeline management, they all need to be integrated and aligned.

Initiatives related to new customer and market growth are built into the strategy, and these initiatives are also built into the plan – either as hard numbers or "upward sensitivities."

These organizations plan not because they like creating plans, but because the planning and alignment process materially improves the things that they care about: leads, conversions, and revenue! Planning holds a special significance, representing a way out of the "dark past" of many companies, where reactivity, politics, finger pointing, and blame culture were the norm.

In practice

Sooner or later the organization will need to ensure it has a fit-for-purpose set of plans, and that these plans are aligned through ongoing processes.

Often it helps to sketch out how the plans fit together and where the gaps are in what is called a planning hierarchy.

Here is an example planning hierarchy:

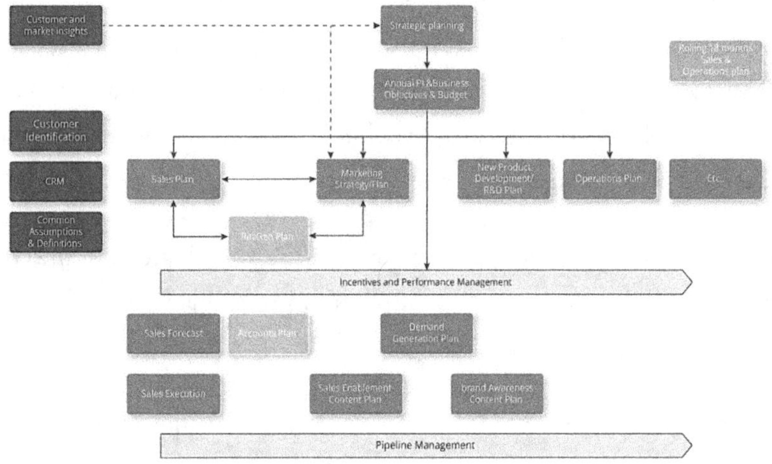

Illustration 7: Planning Hierarchy

At the beginning of your journey, Marketing might be little more than a Sales support function, constantly scrambling to meet the latest demand from the Sales team. The organization might not have a well-defined strategy or strategic plan but a set of general objectives they want to achieve. They might have too many objectives, or original plans are thrown out the window because the Sales strategy is "all money is green" i.e., *we'll sell what we can*. In this scenario, any well intended marketing plan is also thrown out the window.

Coming back to the hierarchy diagram, you can use the diagram as a one-pager talking piece to illustrate this issue. Marketing must rely on the quality of other plans in the organization. If those plans are figurative garbage or not followed, then with what is Marketing supposed to align?

What is the state and integration of plans in your organization? Would building a hierarchy of plans be a useful exercise?

The evolution of Marketing fitting into the planning hierarchy will likely proceed in both a top-down and bottom-up fashion. Top-down in that you will establish the marketing strategy and customer knowledge base that supports the distinct identity and value of Marketing, in line with business objectives. While the bottom-up perspective shows how this knowledge can be used to generate better plans and improved real-time visibility to help manage the pipeline and goals.

In practical terms, the Marketing team will ensure that the Marketing strategy is aligned with and enabling business strategy. It should refer to specific strategic initiatives and go-to-market focus areas. You'll press/align with leadership to give you clarity on which high level objectives you should be pursuing.

In tandem with revenue accountability, the Marketing team will need to create different types of "financialized" plans that map marketing activities to outcomes.

All plans are constrained to some extent by teams and resources. You won't be able to be everything to everyone. Part of the evolving maturity of Marketing will be to understand the relevant constraints and priorities and to communicate these with other teams, clearly stating what Marketing will and won't do.

You'll be expected to understand key priority growth areas for the business and to show how those will be supported by Marketing, along with other potential priorities. This prioritization is an expectation setting and sharing process and will be discussed with the different stakeholder groups such as management, Sales, Business Development, Product, and Global Marketing teams.

For example, your prioritization might be that "A" segments will receive full support, "B" segments will get partial support, and "C" segments might only get ad-hoc "air cover" or be supported from regional or global service centers.

This prioritization represents an ongoing discussion with the business. If more support is required then, by extension, Marketing will require more or different resources.

What data or plans do you use to discuss the right level of resources for the Marketing team at the moment?

There are several tools Marketing teams can use to prioritize initiatives as part of the planning process and regular reviews. The two best known ones are to conduct a regular Impact / Effort review to understand quick wins, big bets, and thankless tasks. Secondly an Impact / Feasibility Matrix can be used to understand where Marketing can have the greatest impact with current resources.

There is a tendency in Marketing (and elsewhere) to always add new tasks to the plan for the new year without taking anything away. The annual planning process is a good time to reflect on what has worked and what hasn't in the last year, and to begin to "stop doing" things that no longer drive results, to leave space for growth initiatives.

B. Budgeting

Descending

For less mature firms, the budget is largely an administrative and back-ward-looking document.

The budget for this year is a function of last year's, irrespective of the change in business activity. For example, a revenue growth target might have been added representing 20% growth, but marketing's budget is only increased 5% or remains flat.

In some cases, the Marketing budget is calculated as a fixed percentage of sales budget. Arbitrary top-down budget cuts such as "everybody take 10% out" are common. There is little confidence in the Marketing budget, since any change in business conditions will mean that the budget is immediately slashed. As a result, the Marketing focus is on hyper short-term activities.

Ascending

The organization has a solid understanding of "activity based" or "driver based" budget calculation as well as the key revenue generating processes while minimizing or optimizing non-revenue generating costs. There is a clear view of ROI and accountability across teams.

The budget is a living document, and the expectation is that it aligns with and is tracked against functional plans, but the two remain separate. Gaps and opportunities to budget are called out separately and worked on collaboratively, rather than popping up as surprises close to year-end. Discrete investment is allocated to developing new customers and markets.

In Practice

The key evolution in terms of budgeting takes Marketing from a cost center to a profit/revenue center.

Marketing will need to change from talking about itself, to talking about how it supports revenue. As we mentioned in the last section, this begins at the planning stage, agreeing what and how Marketing will support the business in terms of activities, and thus the impact on the "cost" side of the budget. The other side of the coin is revenue i.e., how marketing activities translate into revenue.

All too often, marketing activities and budgets are set without a clear view of the ROI expectation. Even today, organizations spend millions of dollars on marketing, yet measure success based on the number of generated leads and are unable to justify or quantify success.

Businesses recognize that they have to invest in marketing, even if the Marketing team is unable to back up the investment with a clear tie-in to revenue growth. It's only a matter of time for this case to persist, and when leadership changes and tough questions are asked heads will roll! Therefore, it isn't a matter of if Marketing will become more systematic and measured, but when.

Too often, we see organizations where Marketing is still perceived as a black box. Because of this, the initial onus is on Marketing to begin working with Finance and the rest of the business to demystify the process of devising and using the marketing budget, tracking results, and adjusting along the way.

In practical terms, this will happen when Marketing can explain the numbers they are using, the levers they are pulling to meet business objectives, and how they relate to planned activities. In the next chapter, we'll discuss processes. Process development and comfort in the robustness of Customer Acquisition, Expansion, and Retention processes will increase the confidence that plans have a stable foundation.

Having the ability to get real-time feedback on execution and make changes as needed, helps avoid surprises at the end of the quarter/year. Fewer surprises over time builds the credibility of the Marketing function and opens the door to future discussions on adding incremental resources.

As the Head of Marketing at a global hardware technology company, the Marketing budget was set as a % of revenue and allocation is based on historical activities without reviews of the return on investment against each activity. Sales had a significant voice on how Marketing budget was spent.

The bulk of the activities focus was on sales support to meet the monthly target instead of adopting a strategic approach to drive long term growth. Marketing was asked by the CEO to create three different versions of budgets to allow last minute adjustments in case the Sales unit needed to deliver more profit to the regional and global offices.

Accruals were used to deliver these financial results at year end leading to a total lack of strategic orientation focused on real business growth. Marketing was just a support function not a strategic unit to drive the business forward. As a result, the company was unable to differentiate itself and thus competed purely on price, relying on constant promotional activities to move the stock.
- Eve Chen

C. Performance Management

"What gets rewarded gets repeated."
"You get what you inspect, not what you expect."
"What gets measured gets managed."

The performance management we'll discuss in this section is purely around goal setting, incentives, and tracking to targets. Later in Chapter 9, we'll talk about detailed KPI's, analytics, and reporting to support decision-making.

Descending

The goals/incentives process conducted in silos is quite opaque and based on how things used to work such as Sales deliver revenue. Such a process leaves Marketing as a support function. As a result, incentives are misaligned, and the organization is pulling in different directions. Individual functions will take action to hit their own objectives, often at the expense of other functions and overall business objectives.

Where top level scorecard measurements do exist, they focus on vanity metrics or generic industry measures that are not connected to what drives the economic engine of the business.

Ascending

Performance goals and measures are aligned with strategy and each other. Goals and measures encourage teams to "win together," and behavior that delivers the right results in the wrong way is dealt with. Real time data is used to track against key performance metrics, and to take corrective action where required. Specific measures have been identified to assess and improve performance of growth initiatives and strategies.

In Practice

It is often said that the Finance team only wants one metric from Marketing which is how much revenue is generated based on how much was spent, i.e., ROI.

The statement above about ROI is a good reality check for Marketers who might otherwise be tempted to bombard the executive team and board with high level measures that don't intuitively link to business results.

The practical reality though is that performance management is more than one metric and will need to be developed in a "top-down" and "bottom-up" fashion. This is in concert with process knowledge, detailed KPI development, alignment of roles, and even detailed driver modeling of the actual levers that can be pulled to affect results.

From a top-down perspective, the aggregate performance management approach, which is often supported by a high-level dashboard and scorecard, should measure how effectively business activity is enabling the strategy and overall plan.

For example, if the strategy is around expanding into new markets, key metrics can be around market penetration rates, gaining market share, new logos, wins against competitors (competitor displacement), NPS/loyalty metrics, and customer advocacy.

If you're looking at more mature markets, then you'll be looking at segment or account penetration and growth (e.g., expanding into new Business Units (BUs) or growing organically - selling more products/services to the same BU), and other customer success related metrics.

Aligning Sales and Marketing to core business goals and understanding what the joint levers they will pull to meet business growth objectives is key. There will be shared metrics and KPIs for cross functional teams - Marketing, Sales, and Customer Success.

The bottom-up perspective is about which detailed analytics and measures (which we will cover in Chapter 9) must be elevated up to leadership dashboards, and potentially to performance measures and incentives. These detailed metrics should indicate the underlying health of the business in the present and a sense of the future, such as a selection of top and bottom funnel metrics.

A practical way to deal with individual detailed metrics and incentivization is to map out who is impacting each step of the buyer's journey both directly and indirectly.

Performance management and goal setting are traditionally the starting point for misalignment between Sales and Marketing.

In one global tech company, planning and performance KPIs were clearly mapped out with cross functional alignment at leadership level. However, high level goals did not translate as equally well across the different teams who were very much siloed - e.g., Sales were focused on revenue and CLV (customer lifetime value), on the other hand, Business Development (lead generation teams) were targeted on qualified opportunities and meetings booked, while Marketing was focused on SQLs (lead generation).

The different teams owned a piece of the buyer journey and the overall sales process; however, they were not speaking the same language. This meant that there were silos and "us vs. them" mentality. The solution to the challenge inevitably lies in a cultural shift, deeper alignment, and breaking down of team siloes and clear revenue accountability across all teams. Sales is a team sport! - Ljubica Radoicic

Concrete Actions:

1. Develop a three-year marketing plan with both short-term and long-term focuses. It needs to speak to how your plan will support the long-term vision and growth of the business.
2. Establish strong relationships with CEO and CFO (the typical roles that perform resource allocations) and present both short-term and long-term strategies and the relevant metrics for them. Make sure long-term growth projects are not being measured the same as short-term strategies.
3. Build a clear scorecard with leading and lagging indicators that will align and communicate KPI metrics for each business goal and corresponding Marketing objectives.

2. Customer/Market

How do you bring the customer or market opportunity to life with planning, budgeting, and performance management?

Collaborative planning and forecasting with customers is an idea that has been around for a while, particularly driven by initiatives such as Sales and Operations Planning (S&OP), and Integrated Business Planning (IBP).

These types of initiatives normalize a process of jointly discussing forward business outlook across functional teams, as well as discussing issues, likely forecast orders and demand for the organization's products and services.

Using professional services firms as an example, it is common to do joint business planning to align on current and future priorities and optimize services spending. Quite often, the client doesn't "know" all the value that the organization has created for it. The planning process also gives the organization insight into the clients' business outlook and which areas they need help with would have the biggest impact.

To make growth possibilities real, they must first be built into a plan. The planning process is a great time to discuss and bake in activity pilots for the next year of GX ideas. Can GX messaging around customer growth be embedded into context, surveys, demand generation, and supported by A/B testing? Part of the budget must be allocated to developing GX opportunities if the firm wants to find new ideas to grow.

A perennial challenge is how to measure the results of new ideas and build these into scorecards and incentives. In terms of GX, you might start with existing measures such as customer churn and retention, on time renewals, account growth, NPS, CSAT, and then seek to understand what effect your GX pilots are having on those measures.

As we alluded to earlier, other scorecard metrics for GX could be around measures of value added to customers. Some firms do this already. For example, if your software saves four hours per user per week, and the customer has X users, then a total yearly time and monetary estimate of value can be made. Firms often have continuous joint improvement programs in place to identify shared opportunities to save time and money on how they deal with each other.

In the future, we can expect an increasingly entrepreneurial approach to Customer Acquisition, Expansion, and Retention with the organization seeking to identify and understand sources of added value to the customer. From there, mobilizing the infrastructure to chase those opportunities down, potentially creating new business models and revenue streams in the process.

3. People

Evolving responsibilities represent a personal journey for the marketer, who might have gotten into the field for the creative aspects of the job and is now increasingly called upon to be a finance person and technologist!

We speak to many marketers who are struggling with the increased responsibilities and expectations placed on them. Some of this reflects the broader period of flux in the roles of Sales and Marketing and Service teams in the new era. Part of this concern is that expectations are getting ahead of investment and capability of Marketing and changes in the organization that support required new ways of working.

For you as a Marketing leader, the direction of travel is clear: increased commercial expectations and responsibilities. Rather than be defensive at B2B Marketing's perceived role as a cost center, recognize Marketing's positions of strength: knowledge of the market and customer, and being the natural function that coordinates product, price, and place to create a seamless buying experience for customers.

Marketing departments suffer from high turnover rates, which impact the Marketing team's ability to effectively service the business. People leave primarily due to lack of growth and development opportunities in organizations and because they don't feel empowered to make decisions. With this in mind, we include turnover as a key metric under GX, since we'd expect it to reduce.

In addition, we'd expect that many of the qualitative and quantitative measures of high-performance teams apply here including: trust, communication, learning and decision making. Marketing leaders need to create a culture of sustainability and growth for their teams, not just themselves.

This also requires a company to proactively engage in employee surveys and feedback to understand what is and isn't working well in the organization. Building a progressive culture with engaged and productive employees is critical. A firm we've worked with recently is doing this well with annual surveys that look at various dimensions - from culture, performance, leadership assessments, to support and career development. Management takes these factors very seriously and uses them to inform specific programs and activities. It's why a firm like this is one of the most loved places to work.

As a counter example, we see firms undertake a culture survey then leadership teams get defensive about and minimize negative results. Perhaps the leadership wants to fix "them" rather than "us," not recognizing that employees respond to the tone and measures from the top, the "walk" more than the "talk."

This is critical for GX as it looks at success more holistically as part of people development. We will be asking people to go above and beyond what they have previously done, and therefore, employees must trust that the firm has good intentions.

Key Takeaways:

- Marketing efforts must be clearly aligned vertically to corporate/business objectives, "horizontally" to Sales and Product, etc., and focused on measurable activities that drive contribution to the business.

- Mature firms have a clear sense of an activity/driver-based approach to budgeting that links the budget to planned business activity, and to strategic investments.

- It is commonly said that the only metric Finance cares about from Marketing is ROI. The challenge for Marketers is to get the right metrics that tell a compelling story about performance and how Marketing is supporting the business.

4

Process

> *"If you can't describe what you are doing as a process,*
> *you don't know what you are doing."*
>
> W Edwards Deming, Engineer, Professor
> and Management Consultant

A study by IDC Market Research concluded that companies lose 20-30% in revenue every year due to inefficiencies. What exactly are these inefficiencies? They include making decisions based on wrong data or acting on old data. It all comes down to data silos. Gartner estimates that making erroneous business decisions based on old or bad data could cost small to mid-sized businesses over $15 million per year in losses on average. This is validated by the *2020 Revenue Generation Maturity Study* where we found among those organizations that believe they have better practice in this area, 77.9% achieved desired revenue performance.

The case *for* process mapping and optimization is that it provides a foundation to understand the work of the firm, focusing it on adding value that leads to revenue and growth, and away from work that doesn't add value or in fact destroys value.

As Marketers, we might be tempted to de-prioritize using data, planning, and process in our decision making. However, to be frank, you can't improve what you can't define.

We've seen again and again that it is virtually impossible to move from constant reactivity and firefighting without a clearly defined process. Developing a structured approach to work is key to moving the Marketing function from being seen purely as a cost center, to becoming a revenue and growth generator.

Process enables *more* creativity due to efficiency, since that leaves incremental time to spend on what generates true value for the organization, rather than spending time dealing with the "bad" of needless variation that only hinders results.

The biggest myth I have encountered while researching creativity, coaching business leaders on how to be more creative, and reflecting on my own creative practice, is that creative people don't use processes. Not true! Early on in my own development, books such as The War of Art by Steve Pressfield, Daily Rituals by Mason Currey, and Creative Confidence by Tom and David Kelley helped legitimize his observation that creativity itself could be viewed as a process. Done well, a process development and optimization initiative can surface constraints that impede performance, leaving more time for new ideas and value-adding conversations that support growth. That's creativity! - Brett Cowell

1. Organizational Growth

One of the big ideas in this book is that the organization can be viewed as being composed of ten foundational capabilities. These core capabilities enable a value chain connecting suppliers and partners, delivering value for customers, and ultimately converting that value into revenue.

This relationship is documented in the Revenue generation Value Chain (RVC) diagram:

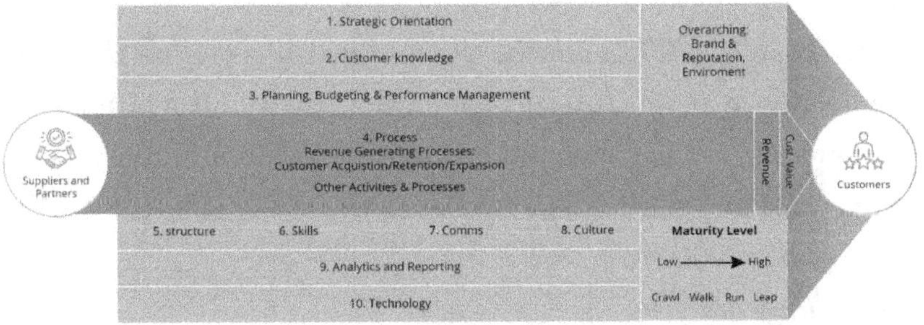

Illustration 3: Revenue Generation Value Chain (RVC)

The ten capabilities contain several constituent processes, but the one called "4. Process" has special significance since it contains the core revenue generating processes of Customer Acquisition, Retention, and Expansion.

To understand the context of revenue generating processes more clearly, you might want to flick forward to the value driver diagram in Chapter 9. Revenue generating processes in the organization pull various "levers" that affect price, quantity, and mix, for example, and affect revenue and profit. The job of process transformation is to bring a laser-like focus to aligning the firm to consistently pull value levers that generate and capture customer value in the form of revenue and revenue growth.

Notice that in the bottom right of the RVC diagram, we refer to Maturity Level (i.e., Crawl, Walk, Run, and Leap). When we talk about the *maturity level* of components in the RVC, we're essentially referring to the level of sophistication, integration, and effectiveness of the practices within each of the 10 components.

Maturity is important because increasing the maturity of a component will increase its effectiveness, and the likelihood that the revenue generation value chain will drive the firm to meet its growth targets.

In this chapter, we'll focus on the revenue generating processes but keep in mind that to improve overall performance, you will want to apply the same process mapping and optimization techniques in the other nine components (the other chapters in Part One).

Descending

When we visit organizations that are early in their transformation journey there's rarely a single process map in sight. People consider "work" in terms of job titles, rather than process, policy, and procedure. Often this lack of process is coupled with poorly defined roles, resulting in employees wearing multiple hats and serving the role of generalist. In this case, the focus is more on getting through the work, rather than being governed by a specific workflow.

Without process, similar situations may be approached with different actions leading to a lack of consistency in outputs or outcomes. A seemingly random approach to similar situations makes it difficult to form trusted relationships between functions in the organization. Work often gets stuck or even lost as it crosses between roles and functions.

Organizational knowledge is rarely documented and the ability to achieve results can easily be disrupted if specific personnel leave or are promoted.

Process inefficiencies and inconsistencies are often exposed directly to the customer such as an inquiry from a contact form is lost or not responded to, while a competitor *does* respond to the same query on their website resulting in a new sale.

Process gaps can be directly linked to and measured as revenue leakage. The sales pipeline has *holes in it* that cost real money.

Efforts to improve work output are often piecemeal or fail due to a lack of common understanding or a single set of processes to serve as the foundation of future improvements.

Ascending

There is a formalized and prioritized effort to not only document key revenue generating processes but to do so in a cross-functional way that builds shared knowledge. Needless to say, the process is the default way that work gets done. The organization takes a proactive approach by implementing practices such as the six-sigma set of process improvement techniques to optimize the customer experience and internal processes.

There is a clear interconnect between revenue generating, strategic, and other planning processes. For example, during the annual planning process, leaders provide clear guidance to all departments on prioritized growth strategies, go-to-market segments, route-to-market decisions, comprehensive revenue targets, as well as the aligned functional plans to achieve them.

Marketing typically uses "playbooks" as a single source of definitions and core processes. Having a playbook allows space and time for value adding discussion and innovation, rather than constant arguing over the rules of the game.

Customer feedback is regularly sought by Sales, Marketing and Customer Success and implemented in process optimization. There are regular interactions with the customer to understand satisfaction with each interaction by using scores like CSAT and often supported by customer success software tools.

In Practice

The work that you and the organization do around revenue generating processes can be chunked up into three sequential phases:

A. Defining and Aligning the Customer Acquisition Process
B. Moving from Funnel to Orbit: Linking Customer Acquisition, Retention, Expansion
C. Optimizing the Organizational Revenue Generating Value Chain

Let's start with Customer Acquisition.

A. Defining and Aligning the Customer Acquisition Process

If there is any single Sales and Marketing process that has received significant focus in recent years, it is the Sales Funnel Management process. This is for good reason, a survey by Vantage Point Performance and the Sales Management Association found that firms that had above average sales process performance had 15-28% higher revenue growth, compared with those having ineffective pipeline management.

At the start of your process improvement journey, there will be at least three versions of the Customer Acquisition process: a Sales team version, a Marketing version, and the customer's experience of the process. There may be no consistent process and thus infinite variations of what gets done and how we talk about the process. When the stages and definitions of the sales process are inconsistent, customer acquisition will also be inconsistent, and thus ineffective, leading to lost revenue.

The first step will be for Marketing to understand the Sales view of the Customer Acquisition and funnel process, to see how Marketing might best align with it. You might find that there is already a well-established process that Marketing can plug into. Or you might find that there is either no process, or a fundamental misalignment between Sales and Marketing, in regards to segments, personas, funnel stages and handoffs. In the case of misalignment, you will need to plan one or more working sessions between Sales and Marketing to define, map, and align processes.

Keep in mind when planning these sessions that part of the value of process mapping is the *journey* to get to the finished maps. For example, by jointly understanding how the firm generates revenue and gaining clarity on roles and responsibilities. As part of the mapping process a RACI (Responsible, Accountable, Consulted, Informed) matrix will typically be created to help build this clarity.

A picture is worth a thousand words and a process can't be improved if it is not documented first. When documenting/drawing your processes as they exist today, be sure to overlay current issues and gaps with sticky notes or their digital equivalent.

Secondly, we've seen again and again how gathering a team around a whiteboard provokes discussion, knowledge sharing, problem identification and a necessary alignment of terminology between departmental functions.

For the marketer, the results of a process mapping and alignment process are often documented in a Marketing Playbook.

Here is a playbook table of contents based on a real example:

What - introduction and purpose

- Business goals and objectives
- Revenue marketing plan
- Marketing strategy and objectives
- Program and game plan

Who - Team

- Team overview and capabilities
- Roles and responsibilities (resource plan)
- RACI and rules of engagement (with other teams)

How - Operational Framework

- Agile Marketing
- Demand & lead generation framework (funnel and lead definitions)
- Program and campaign framework/process

- Content marketing framework
- Lead definition & management
- Data, analytics & reporting (KPIs)
- Marketing tech stack
- Continuous Improvement
- The learning marketing organization

The playbook ensures that all relevant information is in one place, which can also be used to communicate across functions. Given this, it is important to start with the end in mind and use the playbook headings to plan the process mapping and information gathering work. This way you will end up with the information you need to create your Playbook.

When it comes to driving marketing effectiveness and efficiency, I have found that developing and documenting functional and operational playbooks is critical for team clarity and cross functional alignment. Whether it's a startup/SMB with an emerging marketing capability or a complex Global Marketing function, playbooks are essential for operationalizing the strategy and optimizing execution.

I've seen marketers come up with great strategies, but things fall apart in the execution. This is largely because internal processes and teams were not effectively set up - lack of clear processes, roles and responsibilities, documentation, etc.

Developing a playbook is the first step to documenting the status quo and then working cross-functionally to address ownership issues and process gaps. As Marketing as a function continues to go through digital transformation, playbooks become a critical component of the transformation roadmap. - Ljubica Radoicic

Let's get back to the process maps.

The diagram below shows what an integrated Customer Acquisition process might look like.

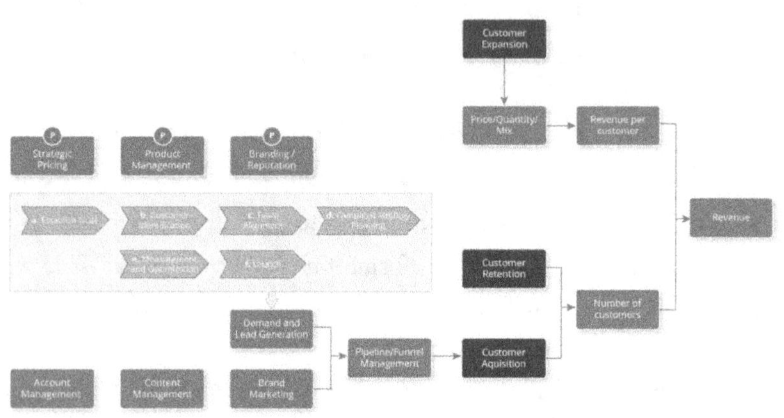

Illustration 8: Example of Customer Acquisition Process

This map only shows the process overview level, and in your process mapping work, you'll dig into pipeline/funnel management and other sub processes to get the complete picture of differences, gaps, and opportunities in current processes.

Next, let's look at the *b. Customer Identification* sub process in more detail. Improved Customer Identification can lead to a fuller pipeline and more closed deals, while also helping avoid non-ideal prospects that would waste organizational time and resources.

Improving Customer Identification involves working on the following four sub-processes:

    i.   Ideal Customer Profile Development

    ii.   Persona Profile Development

   iii.   Persona Messaging

   iv.   Customer Journey Mapping

As we alluded to earlier, these steps match the overall approach to building customer knowledge that we outlined in Chapter 2. By including these steps in the campaign process, you ensure that you're embedding good practices, and can fine-tune customer information for the campaign. Likewise, your Account Based Marketing (ABM) process can be represented on and linked to the overall process maps for Demand/Lead generation.

Once a team creates an effective process in one area, that same knowledge can be used across teams. In this sense we seek not to reinvent the wheel for every business division. And standardized processes make training and technology development across the organization simpler and cheaper too.

If your organization is involved in formal client presentations or Requests for Proposal, you can add another stream to the overall process map to cover that scenario and identify the "best practices." Ensure that you map all the important channels or types of Customer Acquisition that are relevant to your organization, even if we haven't listed them here. Take time to understand the needs behind different current versions of the Acquisition process. Are there critical requirements that need to be documented, or are differences not adding value to the firm or customer?

To further enhance the process maps, you can overlay and discuss other hypothetical situations. For example, Sales requires either materials or collateral from Marketing, or Marketing creates materials with the intent that Sales will use them.

We've seen situations where up to two thirds of marketing content is never used by Sales and yet the Sales team still complains that they don't have the right materials for critical situations. Clearly there is a mismatch, which needs an alignment process around content strategy and management.

Once the basic steps of the process are identified and documented, you can begin to test scenarios and questions against the process, particularly scenarios and questions that bring in the customer's perspective.

You might have market diversification as a specific part of your role objectives, and/or you might decide to immediately tackle diversification after you've proved the benefits of improving acquisition of customers in current focus markets. The implication is that you'll want to ensure, when designing the Customer Acquisition process, that it works both for *current* markets, and for *new* ones. Note: for new markets, you might have additional or different steps in the process which you will want to think through and document. You will return to create and test new processes in the Design stage of AGM.

The stage of streamlining Customer Acquisition as a funnel is already a significant step forward. Although this is only the first of three phases we've talked about, it requires real effort to do well. Don't try to bite off more than you can chew by trying to do all three phases at once. Eat the elephant one slice at a time, as the saying goes (or just leave that elephant alone and do your work in manageable chunks).

B. Moving from Funnel to Orbit: Linking Customer Acquisition, Retention, Expansion

Customer Acquisition has typically been represented by the funnel process; however, we've found that optimizing the funnel is not enough on its own to create a truly leading organization that builds sustainable relationships with customers.

This is why we developed Growth Experience (GX) and "orbits" as a new paradigm for Marketing, Sales, and organizational success, that is win-win-win.

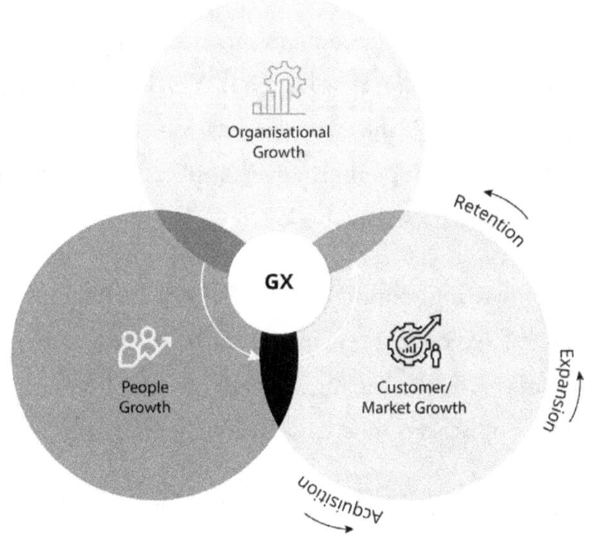

Illustration 2: Customer Orbit of Growth Experience (GX)

In non-Ascending companies, the Sales and Marketing approach and funnel can feel to the customer like "blinding the prospect with technical features, capturing them, and holding the customer hostage." In Ascending Growth, the idea of orbits recognizes that B2B customers are people too. They are free to come, and free to leave. Buying groups expect that messages and interactions will be tailored both to them as a firm, and to them as individuals.

The reality is that there has always been an amount of buying dissonance, even in B2B.

This happens when the reality of dealing with the selected supplier and product/service for the buyer doesn't match up to expectations set during the sales process. This dissonance can be a source of dissatisfaction, leading the buying firm to want to leave just as they've arrived at the same time the "champagne corks" are popping on the Sales side.

It has also long been good procurement practice to *aggregate* and *diversify* spending, practicing supplier development. Yes, your firm might be the main supplier today, but if the customer has done their homework, your buyer will have one or more alternative suppliers that they are keeping warm so not all "eggs are in one basket."

At the time of writing, supply shocks have become more prevalent meaning buyers have often been forced to look beyond their preferred supplier. In some cases, the backup supplier has now become the incumbent, or a new supplier has satisfied a need when others were unable to.

Another procurement trend of publicly rebidding work periodically, or as a result of poor supplier feedback means that a sale is less likely than ever to be a sale for life, particularly with low barriers to exit for many B2B products and services.

All the factors above "pile on" to prove that, although widespread, the funnel was never a satisfactory paradigm for managing buyers/customers anyway. We need to change our paradigm and measures accordingly.

Building a sustainable growth strategy means retaining customers and expanding your relationship with them. The increased measurement of CLV (Customer Lifetime Value) is indicative of this trend, but this still views the customer in terms of dollars first. It is difficult to create innovative value for the customer if you're always thinking about yourself first.

When we talk about core revenue generating processes, we're always talking about a cycle of Acquisition, Retention, and Expansion, rather than a straight line. There is a need to develop new measures that recognize the cyclical nature of the customer's growth experience.

Building an orbit and developing the concept of three intersecting orbits in GX requires top-down and end-to-end thinking that cuts across several functional boundaries.

As you build on the Customer Acquisition process you developed in the last phase (A), you will run new working sessions to add process maps for Customer Retention and Expansion. We'll deal with these more in the section on Customer/Market in this chapter.

We need to start asking and answering some powerful open-ended questions about what really stokes the revenue engine within the organization. This type of question needs to have support and participation not only from leadership, but a cross section of the organization as well to provide a diversity of perspectives.

For example, we might ask "why do customers stay with us?" We might seek to understand what makes a customer for life, and how to identify a prospect that might become a customer for life. Ultimately, we want to build a shared understanding of how to execute for revenue and growth.

The framework that prompts the asking and answering of these questions is the *Revenue Generation Value Chain.*

C. Optimizing the Organizational Revenue Generating Value Chain

The final phase of work in process transformation will be to:

- Understand and optimize processes across the ten components of the RVC
- Optimize the broader set of revenue generating and influencing processes across the organization

Inherent in the RVC is the idea that a mature, integrated, and aligned set of capabilities is the cornerstone of growth.

To make that happen in practice, you will first work through each of the ten components of the RVC to understand the current state and the plan for how those components will look in the future.

You will perform an audit of the current state of these components, including the current state of the integration, alignments, and "handoffs" between components (you will do this in the Data stage of AGM).

Next, in the Design stage of AGM, you will create a new design of each component, then work on designing the right integration and handoffs between them. For example, you'll design how Personas are created and shared/aligned between Sales and Marketing.

The second piece of scaling up the potential process improvement will be to increase the number of revenue generating processes included in the review and optimization process.

The diagram below shows an example of a broader set of processes that influence revenue:

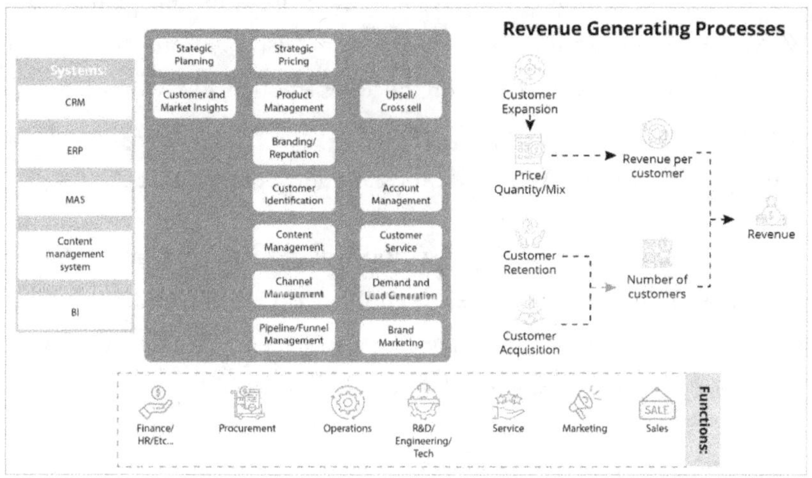

Illustration 9: Revenue Generating Processes

In this diagram, you see not only the core revenue generating processes like Customer Acquisition, Retention, and Expansion, but other processes that also drive revenue including branding and strategic pricing.

Our view is that the Ascending Marketer will play an increasingly strategic and symbiotic role with the leadership team as the oracle for market and customer knowledge, not only for current markets, but for new ones too. This means that Marketers will be able to set and influence the goalposts, which in turn sets the context for Marketing Plans and Customer Acquisition itself.

Another example is Branding/Reputation. This is clearly in the wheelhouse of Marketing and sets the context for revenue generation and growth. However, the brand may or may not be under your control depending on the structure of the organization; it might be managed globally, while you are working regionally or at a country level.

Branding has a natural but indirect relationship to revenue generation. We've chosen not to focus on the brand in this book, but that doesn't mean that it isn't part of GX or the RVC model! Ask yourself if the processes you're developing align with and deliver on the overarching brand promise or not. Where are the gaps and opportunities?

The point here is that the organization will need to continue to better its understanding of what drives revenue, incorporating and optimizing a broader set of processes and aligning a wider set of stakeholders both inside and outside the organization to drive sustainable growth.

Concrete Actions:

- Create operational and activity-based playbooks for your function/team and blueprint key processes
- Perform Journey mapping
- Conduct regular process reviews to optimize operational efficiency and drive better results (get team members to complete Six Sigma training)
- Consider adopting and implementing Agile methodology

2. Customer/Market

Presumably the foundation of your win-win with the customer is that the customer gets value from your product and service, and you get value from the customer. It costs less to keep a customer than to acquire one and from the buyer's side, all other things being equal, it is easier to expand a relationship that is already working than to find something new.

As we've said above, the moment you acquire a customer, you must begin to retain them. Although the renewal date might be some time in the future, first impressions matter, and a customer unable to get value from a product won't renew. Instead of retention being a milestone, treat it as a daily equation that is heightened by certain moments of truth such as issues with the product or service, or victories supported by the product or service.

Yet the customer retention process is often separated from discussions of revenue, frequently due to organizational structure and differing goals and incentives.

In fact, many elements of customer retention share the same characteristics as customer acquisition: getting feedback, understanding the customer's real needs, what keeps them satisfied enough to stay with you, or unsatisfied enough to leave. You might also run campaigns to target at-risk customers or update your personas to reflect what real customers say about what they do or do not like or need.

We sometimes ask the question of groups "Which is more important, customer value or customer satisfaction?" A hearty debate normally ensues. It can be useful to inject some of this debate into your process reviews, and while getting the organization on the path to growth centricity. In reality customer value and customer satisfaction are related, and both are important but do not always have the same drivers or importance in every situation.

Customer Expansion

Customer Expansion incorporates approaches such as upselling and cross selling to maximize revenue per customer. This is both in the Acquisition process, and later post-purchase, including total lifetime customer revenue.

Studying customer or persona needs can help identify areas for cross sell, whether this is from existing products and services or from future ones.

As with the other two processes, customer feedback can be helpful insight when designing promotions and understanding what turns a good customer into a great one.

For example, leading companies pursue the following approaches to customer expansion:

- Training customer success and services teams to identify growth opportunities within existing accounts as part of regular customer support calls (e.g., Technology companies).
- Conducting health checks and maturity assessment of customer accounts to identify opportunities for optimization and value growth.
- Understanding customer behavior and trigger points for specific expansion messaging such as product usage in SaaS companies. Or the stages of customer lifecycle and specific buying signals.

How will you change existing processes or add new ones to capture GX opportunity?

There is a clear opportunity to change up the conversation with customers in a way that incorporates growth across both demand generation and branding activities. This might involve meeting with customers to flesh out what growth means to them, then feeding this back into the customer acquisition process.

Another starting point is to consider the move from product selling to solution selling. In this scenario the process for engaging potential customers will be different, both digitally and in-person. For solution selling, the firm must be able to demonstrate knowledge of the customer and the customer's business/industry. The implication for the firm is that, at a minimum, it must update expectations, skills and processes surrounding customer engagement.

For example, initial meetings with the customer might be structured to discuss the customer's situation, business outlook and broader issues, rather than simply the features of the firm's product.

Many professional services firms have sophisticated account management policies for both existing and "must win" accounts. A consulting firm, for example, will begin to target individuals in these must-win future accounts. They'll provide free advice, materials, coaching, help with presentations, and even free services to build the relationship, and show that "we're here for the long haul."

How can these examples be applied to your situation?

Which models of Customer Retention and Expansion can you find from competitors or different industries that move the customer and growth experience forward?

3. People

For leaders, the people aspect of GX is becoming more data-driven and cross-functional. Being involved in cross-functional and end-to-end process development is a great way to learn these skills since it builds knowledge of how the work of different functions fits together to drive a desirable outcome.

It has certainly been an eye opener for us to be involved in cross-functional, process-driven projects. Once participants from the different functions build trust and start working towards a common goal, you're able to objectively acknowledge the gaps in the current system and devise new ways to support improved performance and growth.

For teams, the initial phase of process development involves clarifying their roles, getting rid of some "hats" they wear, and developing team partnership that extends across different aspects of the business.

Key Takeaways:

- The business cannot sustainably improve and grow unless core revenue generating processes are understood, followed, and optimized.

- For many organizations, a lot of the initial activity and value will come from first aligning the funnel, then by moving on to more advanced ideas like orbits and Revenue Generation Value Chain optimization. Don't try to do too much at one time.

- Don't underestimate the value of creating a process map to bring teams together and build shared understanding and trust. These benefits will extend in time way beyond the several days you'll put aside for process mapping.

5

Structure

"Architecture studies not structure in itself, but the effect of structure on the human spirit."

Geoffrey Scott, Architectural Historian

All too often, great strategy is derailed by poor execution.

Instead of promoting focus, alignment, and functional specialization, poor structure can set the organization up for failure, creating silos and competing objectives that hinder the ability to meet objectives. The firm's energy becomes focused on other things like internal politics rather than on external customers and competitors. The *2020 Revenue Generation Maturity Study* showed us exactly that. Those considered themselves to have less than ideal practice when it comes to how well defined and structured their human resources are in their organizations, 63.8% performed poorly in their revenue results in the last 12 months.

The biggest misconception about structure is that it reduces agility and creates unnecessary bureaucracy. Instead, an appropriately designed structure with clear roles and responsibilities can set people free to be their best.

Things change. Companies are still grappling with the ongoing impact of Digital Transformation and Customer Experience that continue to impact the balance and nature of work between Sales and Marketing and beyond. Strategy will evolve to include new growth initiatives and exploration of the possibilities created by GX, and these will require evolution in structure and roles. Not all of those evolutions are clear now, but there is no one size that fits all when structuring for growth.

Even today, after decades of investment in other growth initiatives like Innovation and M&A, companies still grapple with how to execute them properly, and the majority fail to deliver business value.

Learnings from Innovation and M&A projects underscore the need to continue to experiment with the right processes and structures, and to be mindful of culture to help realize "bets" on future growth of all kinds.

This chapter is the first of four that will explicitly deal with people. You might wonder why we've waited until Chapter 5 to get onto the topic!

The reason is that we've been following a "top down," sequential approach. We started with Strategy (the big what and why), moved on to Customer (for whom), devised the Plan (where) and then talked about the Processes (how) that deliver the work.

We need all that information to truly understand what the required work will look like both now and over the next 3-5 years.

In this chapter, we'll take it to the next level of detail and look at the structural elements and roles required to support go-to-market strategy, and core revenue generating processes. In this next chapter we'll look at the people and skills required.

1. Organizational Growth

Descending

Descending organizations might not have a separate Marketing team, with tasks led by the CEO or COO, and performed by junior level employees who predominantly help organize company events.

There are often no formal job or skills descriptions, and resources are frequently redirected to other tasks. Job promotion is often based on years of service, rather than experience or performance, and personnel are often swapped in and out of Marketing. There is little if any sense of functional cohesion, continuous improvement, or pride.

In the case where there is a Marketing leader, they mostly perform tactical functions, "wasting" their leadership skills. Crawl organizations are often under-resourced and in fire-fighting mode. There is little ability to be strategic or build momentum around sustainable growth. "All hands-on deck, all the time" is not a sustainable strategy and key personnel often burn out or leave.

Ascending

Ascending organizations have their roles and responsibilities well defined. The organizational structure is set up to support strategic, business, and functional plans. The organization takes a longer (3-5 year) view of structure, so they are not constantly restructuring due to what's in "fashion" or from not incorporating what were foreseeable future needs or drivers at the time of the previous restructure.

There are clear expectations set for which activities Marketing will and will not support, and those are matched to the current level of resources and skill. Organizational effort is matched to priority segments.

There is a clear skill inventory mapped out based on current and future business needs and this is maintained, reviewed, and updated periodically. The structure and job descriptions also support the needs of lead generation and management as well as customer lifecycle management.

Roles are designed to support the Revenue Generation Value Chain. Structure and roles support the activities and processes for revenue generation and pipeline management. There is a culture of continuous improvement, and procedural or structural obstacles are analyzed and systematically removed.

There is both a functional pride and organizational "win-together" mindset among personnel. There is a viable career path in Marketing, including leadership, CEO, and potentially beyond.

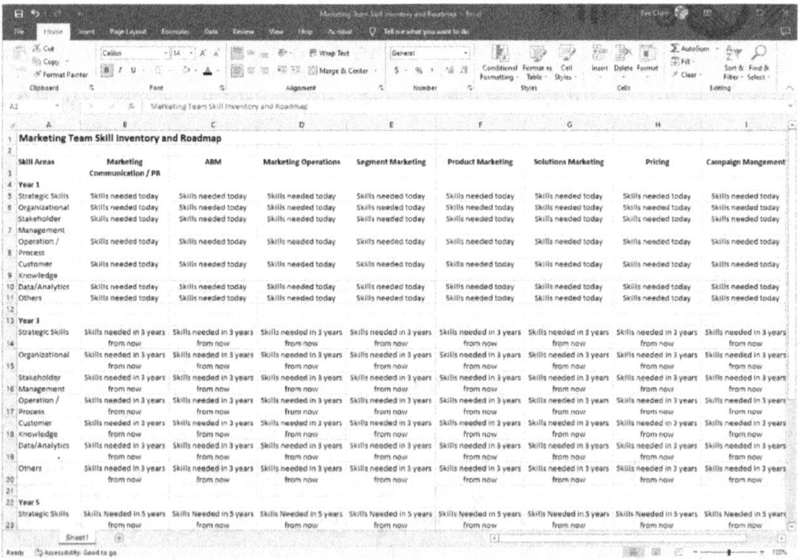

Marketing Team Skill Inventory and Roadmap

Skill Areas	Marketing Communication / PR	ABM	Marketing Operations	Segment Marketing	Product Marketing	Solutions Marketing	Pricing	Campaign Mangement
Year 1								
Strategic Skills	Skills needed today	Skills needed today	Skills needed today	Skills needed today	Skills needed today	Skills needed today	Skills needed today	Skills needed today
Organizational	Skills needed today	Skills needed today	Skills needed today	Skills needed today	Skills needed today	Skills needed today	Skills needed today	Skills needed today
Stakeholder Management	Skills needed today	Skills needed today	Skills needed today	Skills needed today	Skills needed today	Skills needed today	Skills needed today	Skills needed today
Operation / Process	Skills needed today	Skills needed today	Skills needed today	Skills needed today	Skills needed today	Skills needed today	Skills needed today	Skills needed today
Customer Knowledge	Skills needed today	Skills needed today	Skills needed today	Skills needed today	Skills needed today	Skills needed today	Skills needed today	Skills needed today
Data/Analytics	Skills needed today	Skills needed today	Skills needed today	Skills needed today	Skills needed today	Skills needed today	Skills needed today	Skills needed today
Others	Skills needed today	Skills needed today	Skills needed today	Skills needed today	Skills needed today	Skills needed today	Skills needed today	Skills needed today
Year 3								
Strategic Skills	Skills needed in 3 years from now	Skills needed in 3 years from now	Skills needed in 3 years from now	Skills needed in 3 years from now	Skills needed in 3 years from now	Skills needed in 3 years from now	Skills needed in 3 years from now	Skills needed in 3 years from now
Organizational	Skills needed in 3 years from now	Skills needed in 3 years from now	Skills needed in 3 years from now	Skills needed in 3 years from now	Skills needed in 3 years from now	Skills needed in 3 years from now	Skills needed in 3 years from now	Skills needed in 3 years from now
Stakeholder Management	Skills needed in 3 years from now	Skills needed in 3 years from now	Skills needed in 3 years from now	Skills needed in 3 years from now	Skills needed in 3 years from now	Skills needed in 3 years from now	Skills needed in 3 years from now	Skills needed in 3 years from now
Operation / Process	Skills needed in 3 years from now	Skills needed in 3 years from now	Skills needed in 3 years from now	Skills needed in 3 years from now	Skills needed in 3 years from now	Skills needed in 3 years from now	Skills needed in 3 years from now	Skills needed in 3 years from now
Customer Knowledge	Skills needed in 3 years from now	Skills needed in 3 years from now	Skills needed in 3 years from now	Skills needed in 3 years from now	Skills needed in 3 years from now	Skills needed in 3 years from now	Skills needed in 3 years from now	Skills needed in 3 years from now
Data/Analytics	Skills needed in 3 years from now	Skills needed in 3 years from now	Skills needed in 3 years from now	Skills needed in 3 years from now	Skills needed in 3 years from now	Skills needed in 3 years from now	Skills needed in 3 years from now	Skills needed in 3 years from now
Others	Skills needed in 3 years from now	Skills needed in 3 years from now	Skills needed in 3 years from now	Skills needed in 3 years from now	Skills needed in 3 years from now	Skills needed in 3 years from now	Skills needed in 3 years from now	Skills needed in 3 years from now
Year 5								
Strategic Skills	Skills Needed in 5 years from now	Skills Needed in 5 years from now	Skills Needed in 5 years from now	Skills Needed in 5 years from now	Skills Needed in 5 years from now	Skills Needed in 5 years from now	Skills Needed in 5 years from now	Skills Needed in 5 years from now

Illustration 10: Example of a skill inventory matrix

In Practice

We've all heard that structure follows strategy. Yet structural design remains, like many things, a combination of art and science. Just because a particular structure or design approach works at one place, doesn't mean that the structure will be effective elsewhere. It is the principles of design that tend to remain the same. It may be that your firm is not ready to build a "leading class marketing structure" on Day 1. You might have to do more by rearranging and improving what you have today, to get a larger budget for your ideal team in the future. New roles may also need to be piloted on a small scale before being ramped up to a bigger team.

As we've already said, the most important first step is to understand the go-to-market approach and to define how Marketing will support that. Any benefits of structural tweaks will quickly be lost if Marketing and Sales are working on different things.

"While working with a technology company, the Sales team structured their resources based on the size of the market with the following segments: Enterprise (direct sales), SMB (resell/VAR channel), and consumers (retail channel). Marketing resources were structured to align with the Sales team, and a dedicated Marketing Manager was assigned for each segment. When the organization moved from selling hardware to selling solutions, the Marketing resources were also restructured to both ensure lead generation and that customer marketing activities aligned with sales activities.

This immediately became a challenge due to lack of resources when sales dipped during the transition. As a result, I brought in an offshore team and six strategic marketing agencies to fill the needed roles.

These external resources were built into the formal structure of my organization. Each one was clear on their goals and how they would work hand in hand with the Sales division. Sales was able to go directly to these resources with me acting as the project manager, ensuring work requests were delivered within budget and the tasks were aligned with the business goals." -Eve Chen

"I've seen Sales teams set up by region and country meaning that they were selling across multiple segments, industries, and buying groups. For Marketing to align with Sales, the field marketing team was also aligned to support multiple countries. However, this was challenging because the Marketing team was small and couldn't support the sales team in each country. This created a lot of tension and pressure on Marketing. It also meant that there was no clear line of sight with the customer. Sales were purely focusing on the next product sale vs. positioning themselves as a strategic advisor. Subsequently, the Sales team reorganized to focus on customer segments across multiple geos and marketing followed. This was a positive move since it meant that the lines between Customer, Sales, and Marketing were closely aligned.

At a later firm, Sales and Marketing were closely aligned across different customer segments (Ent, Mid-Market, SMB) and there was clear prioritization of geos based on identified growth opportunities and digital maturity. This removed a lot of friction from the Sales and Marketing relationship and ensured that the teams were better positioned to drive growth in markets with the greatest opportunity." - Ljubica Radoicic

Structural design often involves answering practical questions, such as: Does the firm's strategy require inside or outside Sales? Does it require "hunters" or "farmers?" Content and new web support? Alternative compensation plans? What about new territories? And ultimately: What does your strategy require to be successful?

As a Marketing leader, you'll often have to deal with the aftermath of implementing multi-country marketing service centers. The organization will need to find the local resources needed to make this work, which is almost always more resources than the most pie-in-the-sky scenario suggests. Multi-country and global service centers can and do work for certain tasks at certain times.

The pilot approach can be effective in proving certain structural decisions such as adding new roles.

"At a previous firm, key growth was to expand into new markets and acquire new accounts. With marketing generating leads there was a need for sales to accelerate growth and deploy an SDR/BDR team that would support outbound prospecting and inbound lead qualification.

With the company operating in a complex industry with enterprise sales, they mostly relied on the sales reps to do prospecting themselves. The Sales team did not have the expertise or motivation to do this kind of work and would default to existing accounts and existing relationships. There was a need for sales specialization - introduce a new team that was skilled at breaking into new accounts, building, and nurturing relationships, prospecting and filling the sales funnel with qualified opportunities.

The company tried a similar approach by outsourcing to a third party but failed due to the complexity of the product and the level of technical understanding needed to have a credible conversation. I was able to build a business case for getting this kind of team inhouse. We started small and had a team of three. In the first three months they generated a multimillion-dollar pipeline. In two years' time the team grew to a team of nine reps in Asia Pacific and similar teams were set up in other regions with a new function of 50+ reps globally." - Ljubica Radoicic

The reality is that most structures have matured by necessity rather than by design. Perhaps the free-flowing way of working when the organization was smaller no longer works when the organization scales up, and a structural solution with improved governance is required.

You should take the time to include analysis of structures in your audit or strategy development process. Even though your firm might not have the appetite for structural change in the immediate future, it is important to at least align Sales and Marketing on how a more ideal state might function.

How to build Sales and Marketing Alignment

No one will dispute that building Sales and Marketing alignment is one of top challenges for organizations of all sizes. It starts with how teams are structured, aligned, and how Marketing demonstrates value to the Sales process, which is to get more meetings, higher value deals and to close more sales.

Marketing is often removed or not part of this process, so it gets sidelined because it doesn't have a true partnership with Sales. Sales and Marketing teams are often siloed and focused on their own agendas. We've seen Marketing teams focus on long-term brand building programs based around thought leadership/PR, events and lead generation which have little or no immediate impact on sales and revenue. Therefore, Marketing is seen as irrelevant, siloed and removed from customers and the sales process.

True alignment comes with both teams having a deep understanding of where the other drives the value creation process for the customers.

Misalignment can also be caused when the Sales and Marketing teams have different KPIs and objectives. Marketing teams mostly focus on lead generation, whereas Sales focuses on opportunities. What Marketing defines as a "lead", or "MQL/SQL" is not how Sales sees a lead. So, there are some key structure, operational, and success metrics that must be defined by both teams.

True alignment begins with both teams understanding how they can work together to win business. We've heard both positive and negative sentiment toward Marketing, but the bottom line is that often the Sales teams and Sales leaders do not know how to work with or leverage Marketing for success.

The rubber really hits the road when applying Account Based Marketing (ABM) practices. This is where the Sales team gets truly aligned and works closely with the Marketing team to meet certain goals. That is, breaking into an account where there are no existing relationships, broadening reach into other departments or establishing overarching relationships with C level executives of an account if previous relationships had been with middle managers or even users.

Piloting an ABM program and adopting the best practice for program design and rollout can be a great starting point for building alignment and proving the relationship between Sales and Marketing can be a win/win for both teams. Taking a step back from this to look at a bigger picture opportunity - Sales and Marketing alignment starts with setting strategy and objectives at the business levels and aligning sales/marketing goals in a quantifiable way. All too often, we've seen Sales teams lack a well-documented plan. There might be a plan at a global or regional level, but not detailed plans for key market segments so it becomes difficult to join forces because the Sales team is not clear where the opportunities are. This is why it's often up to the CMO to be that driver of change, facilitate conversations, and ask tough questions.

The best Sales and Marketing alignment I experienced was at a technology company I joined as their Channel Marketing Manager. I had to work closely with the Channel Sales team of twenty, while I was the only marketing manager they interacted with. In the first 30 days, I sat down with each of the channel sales one-on-one to understand their business, their pain points, and their goals. From there I established that I needed them to help me to help them, that we had to work together to grow the channel business.

The first thing I did was write a 100-page channel marketing playbook that documented all the marketing activities that improve our resell business and partner relationships. This was also to ensure the business knew how to conduct the channel marketing if I was hit by a bus! I developed a financial portfolio approach to engage with our channel partners. I made sure I launched it with our channel sales so they understood this innovative approach would help them strengthen their partnerships.

I was tasked to manage a $1.3m Channel Marketing Budget, more than the head of Marketing at the time who managed the CAPEX marketing budget. I developed clear guidelines on how funding could be made available to individual channel sales for their partners to improve market penetration in their territories. I worked with each channel sales as partners and we reviewed our goals and progress monthly.

This really helped them embrace me as part of their team. As a result of our alignment, we doubled the business and achieved every quarterly target. It was phenomenal, and I would go out to karaoke or ten pin bowling with the channel sales teams to celebrate our success.

They didn't just treat me as a colleague, we were like a family. It was a wonderful feeling and kept us winning in the business. When the VP of Sales from Singapore interviewed me, she made the comment that I was very loyal to the firm. I told her, "I am not loyal to the firm, I am loyal to my colleagues. Without them, the firm has nothing." She was surprised by what I said but I meant every word. That Sales and Marketing alignment while I was the Channel Marketing Manager made me feel all the hard work was worth it. I was working 70+hours a week not to get a pay rise, but to see my team succeed!" - Eve Chen

Concrete Actions:

- Prioritize the education of Sales as a strategic partner.
- Provide clarity on rules of engagement between Sales and Marketing. This can be achieved through the clear articulation of roles and responsibilities, KPIs, goals, revenue alignment in the format of a Playbook.
- Develop and champion structure tweaks to allow alignment between teams based on the customer journey.
- Build processes that involve everyone, so Sales and Marketing aren't living on separate planets. ABM programs can help to achieve that.
- Review the structure, resources, and metrics periodically to ensure optimal alignment and outcomes.

2. Customer/Market Growth

As we've mentioned already, the first step of structural alignment is getting Sales and Marketing teams aligned by customer segment/GTM. That will already enable a more tailored approach to each customer group while also identifying ways to better serve specific customer needs.

Another common question is how the organization should support moving from product to solution selling in terms of roles and structure. We know that existing teams might not have the skillsets or experience of working in a broader solution context. The team might need to be retrained, replaced, or potentially supplemented with outside industry experts in the key industries you're targeting. Non-key industries might rely on retraining existing personnel with Sales Enablement toolkits.

The broader structural challenge of growth is to answer three related questions:

- What new roles, if any, should the firm create to optimize growth?
- How should we organize growth focused activities and roles optimally to avoid double efforts and cross purposes?
- How does the CMO role fit into all of this?

Let us share some thoughts on these questions now.

Underlying challenges including current levels of skill, scope, focus, coordination, and capacity, as well as the specifics of individuals have driven the desire to create new growth roles.

For example, we've advocated the need to focus. Eventually, what you're not focusing on today will grow to a size that will require allocating resources to pursue it. The type of resource that thrives on this new business generation is likely different from those who farm your existing key segments, perhaps leading to the creation of a role or team with different metrics.

Sometimes the issue with growth is misalignment and opportunities falling between the cracks during handoffs between functions. Creating a new role can give that person the mandate to work cross-functionally. Examples of that include the creation of the Chief Customer Officer (CCO) role and new roles and structures such as customer care teams or managers, customer advisory boards, and a range of customer journey, and design roles. You may also create roles for process improvement specialists and project managers.

There has been a recent trend to add the Chief Revenue Officer (CRO) and/or Chief Growth Officer (CGO) roles, often reporting directly to the CEO.

These new roles highlight a perennial challenge with business structure: how to prevent the new roles from cannibalizing, disrupting, or destroying the core business and existing relationships? Part of the answer to this is ensuring clarity on who will work on what. It also helps if roles and accountabilities are clear in the existing organization. Adding more fuel to a mess usually results in a bigger mess.

Looking at a big picture example of organizational growth, it's possible your firm will choose to incubate new businesses by creating new (temporary) business units for them, which might be rolled back into the main organization at a later stage. This type of example highlights how the "right" answer of how to structure marketing is not one size fits all. In some cases, economies of scale, scope, and skill will point towards the centralization of Marketing. In other cases, there will be a legitimate need for a differentiated structure and service level.

3. People Growth

We enjoyed quite a hearty debate between us around flexibility vs. foresight in designing and managing organizational structure.

The case for flexibility is the idea that some of the typical functional structures put in place in organizations are relics of the Industrial Revolution. Well into the 21st century, we're still constantly talking about alignment. Instead of always continuing to ask, "how do we align?" and looking for a panacea for historic and well-known structural issues, shouldn't we first ask, "what needs to be done, and then what structural ideas allow us to achieve that, balancing cost, quality, responsiveness?"

The case for foresight starts with recognizing that many organizations simply don't plan well. Instead of expecting the team to change at a moment's notice, shouldn't we plan correctly and design roles thoughtfully, thereby eliminating constant unnecessary and debilitating reactivity? Simply calling something "agile" doesn't mean it is. And the label can be a cover for a litany of poor management practices, including the expectation that employees will deal with changing priorities while wearing multiple hats.

Structure is more than a headcount and reporting line exercise and is yet another area where an Ascending Marketer will need to invest the time (and get input) to buffer the team from constant changes and set them up for success. What is certain is that the Marketing leader of today and tomorrow will need to be more than simply a great marketer. They need to be a well-rounded leader used to working across traditional functional boundaries to unlock growth.

That vision of the future might be miles away from where you are now. Perhaps the first steps are to establish an identity for the Marketing function and for yourself, educating your peers and the leadership team on the benefits of Marketing and how it operates as a function. This will almost certainly involve making the personal leap as a leader from talking about the internal nuts and bolts of the Marketing department, to talking about how Marketing not just supports but drives business outcomes.

Growing companies help attract the best talent and retain what they already have. Pursuing GX as a philosophy is a powerful *signaling* device to those *inside* the organization as much as those *outside* of it. There is no way around it, growth is a key pillar of meaning for most people (as are community and contribution). Of course, it is possible to grow when things are difficult, though sometimes you'll realize that the company hasn't been treating you well in the good times and wants your loyalty in the bad times. The lesson of *caveat emptor* applies equally to work.

It is our belief that the Ascending CMO is, in principle, well positioned to move into a larger growth role ("GXO") or to the CEO spot. The first prerequisite for this move is that the CMO continues to demonstrate the ability to drive economic results not only within Marketing but for the business overall, driving a holistic approach to growth.

Many CMOs that have come up through the Marketing ranks or moved into Marketing lack this vision because they lack a holistic view of business and customer. Secondly, the CMO must broaden their leadership skills and ability to work cross functionally. Not all CMOs today are right for non-marketing roles that require a specific caliber of leader. To be successful, they will need a high level of acumen and strategic thinking. This can be developed via coaching. This is why CMOs that want to become true GXOs, face a learning and growth path. CMOs need to build acumen around establishing the vision, and delivering business results both today and tomorrow.

Key Takeaways:

- Structure should follow strategy and go-to-market approach.

- True alignment starts with both the Sales and Marketing teams understanding how they can work together to win business.

- Although we've made the case for "Marketers for world domination" in this book, the reality is that not all marketers will want, or be cut out for Executive roles. Since GXO and CRO roles are a new idea they've yet to wash through the entire cross section of B2B organizations. While the need to work across silos is clear, there is yet to be a silver bullet answer to what works everywhere, and there likely won't ever be! Firms will need to optimize structures based on their own situations and in some cases through piloting different approaches.

- Being agile and proactive is important for optimal structural set up as the business evolves and market shifts happen, teams need to be adaptive and resilient.

6
Skills

"The only skill that will be important in the 21st century is the skill of learning new skills. Everything else will become obsolete over time."

Peter Drucker, Management Educator and Author

If you want to "do things differently and do different things," then the team will not only need the right skillset but also the right mindset to make growth happen. The ability to cultivate a particular mindset *is* arguably the most critical skill an employee can develop! The *2020 Revenue Generation Maturity Study* found that of those considered themselves with above the average practice, 75% achieved their revenue goals.

This tells us that you not only need to "get the right people on the bus in the right seats" *once*, but you'll need to let personnel on and off the bus at different stages. Things change and that means the firm, its customers and markets change. And, as you heard in the last chapter, some of these folks will likely be a combination of third parties, consultants, and personnel.

Given this, you'll need to continue the work you did last chapter about structure as well as the chapters prior.

Without a clear view on business objectives, go-to-market and planning, how will you determine which type of skills will be required to support, for example, solution selling, or market differentiation?

Without an understanding of process and structure then roles and responsibilities will remain unclear. Skills and resources might be duplicated between teams or represent a gap where one function is assuming another is doing the work.

A common example of duplication is around reporting and analysis. That is, valuable resources are being taken up in several teams producing similar reports with slightly different formats, when that reporting effort could be shared. Sharing also reduces the risk of different teams having different numbers for core metrics such as revenue.

Another example of duplication is found in market intelligence. Often, various functions within the organization will be producing or buying market intelligence from different sources or consultancies. Apart from the cost, this results in functions getting diverse information, forming differing assumptions, and pulling in different directions. This type of issue is particularly relevant to Marketing, who will increasingly position themselves as the oracle for customer and market knowledge.

To get skills right, you need to have a clear view of "what's changing." This is the "From:To" we've been talking about; building the right skills to support the requirements of tomorrow, not just today.

Typically, Marketing leaders will perform a skills assessment. The results build a picture of the full set of skills required tomorrow, then compare that across teams with what is in place today. A prioritized list of gaps, sometimes represented as a heatmap, is then produced. From there a strategy around skills will be developed to fill the gaps through things like training, new hires, or external agencies as so on.

The totality of skills required will cover both technical, functional, and people skills often referred to as "hard" and "soft" skills.

As a baseline, technical and functional skills will include those required to work with the current and future marketing technology (Martech) stack at the company. As B2B Marketing has moved towards demand generation, a yin-yang of skills is required: the ability to communicate clearly and craft written content, and at the same time a comfort with interpreting and analyzing data. Other team skills such as knowledge of Search Engine Optimization (SEO) have become the norm.

In most roles, critical thinking, problem solving, and creativity have become increasingly important. These skills bridge the traditional divide between "hard" and "soft" skills and are an important set of "meta" skills that can be applied to individual tasks as well as in developing perspectives and ideas related to disrupting the bigger picture.

As we've mentioned, industry knowledge might be a critical gap if the firm is basing its growth plan on expansion into new markets. Likewise, personnel in both Sales and Marketing, will need to be comfortable engaging the customer around their business issues, and the business benefits delivered by a solution, not just the features of the product/service.

With remote working, initiative and self-management have become more important than ever. Personnel, whether working from office or home, need to move from a "9-5" mindset to an outcomes-based mindset. In principle, staff able to do this well will be able to enjoy the benefits of increased flexibility, rather than just working more hours. Expectations around collaboration and inclusiveness have also increased so that it's not just the "what" of work, completing the assigned tasks, but the "how" that is important, working effectively across teams.

Skills go hand-in-hand with behaviors (and therefore culture). Personnel that have lower levels of maturity might have a "not my job" mentality, where employees are unwilling to learn, grow, or help others outside their narrow job description. Moving beyond these challenges involves a holistic approach of looking at structure, roles and responsibilities, skills, and levels of resourcing, as well as leadership behaviors.

Firms at higher levels of maturity such as "Leap" will begin to see their people and integrated skills as a competitive advantage, and back this up through an enlightened approach to employee learning and development. Firms at this level will have a far better ability to retain top talent as well. In fact, 86% of millennials indicated that they would be less likely to leave their current position if their employer offered training and development.

1. Organization Growth

Descending

Firms tend to lack both formal role and skill descriptions, as the two are interlinked. They also tend to lack formal process definitions. The combination of these three things means that performance is inconsistent, and the organization will be hampered not only on growth, but on day-to-day plan execution.

These organizations tend to lack a formalized Learning and Development structure or budget. Career and succession planning are minimal.

Ascending

The firm has drilled down its strategy and competitive positioning into capabilities, and the concept of core/differentiating is well understood. Capabilities at the organizational level are mapped to departmental and individual capabilities. There is a view of skills required today and those required in 3-5 years' time to support both strategic and market evolution.

There is a well-established Learning and Development structure and strategy in place. Investment in employees via training is a point of pride but is only one of the many methods used to help enrich employees. Others include formal career development, stretch roles, and even paid time to work on personal or charitable projects.

There is an open, knowledge sharing culture in the organization, which also includes mechanisms such as peer correction of those that try to hoard knowledge useful to others. Knowledge is shared across the organization. It is common for personnel in Marketing to implant or intern in the Sales team and receive the same training to further smooth working relationships.

All customer facing staff are extensively trained and understand the end-to-end customer journey beyond their immediate role.

Almost every single employee will have received some combination of continuous improvement, creativity and/or problem-solving training.

In Practice

"Hire for attitude, train for skill" – Herb Kelleher, Co-founder, and former CEO Southwest Airlines

You'll rarely start with a completely blank slate when building a Marketing team. Instead, you'll inherit or already have an existing team in place, and be looking to understand the skill gap between today and what you'll need in the future. That future state is based on the business strategy and growth plans. The gap you identify feeds into a skills development plan or strategy.

Knowing the required skills and team is one of the key areas where a Marketing leader can shape the effectiveness and efficiency of strategy and development. Often, Marketing leaders struggle with hiring and developing talent because they don't know how to consistently connect talent and strategy.

They look at things at a more tactical or task level, resulting in team structures that are misaligned with business growth and future focus. The structures were very much at the *crawl* or *walk* stage, but the team skills and mindset needed to be at the *run* and *leap* stages. This means hiring and building a team for tomorrow, today!

While people were hired for current experience or expertise, many Marketing leaders struggle with transitioning the existing personnel into a different team culture and mindset. Team members were forced to challenge their own experience and status quo. Sometimes in doing so, the business sets them up for failure.

"I joined a company where Marketing was focused on PR, creative/digital, and events. It was very tactical and channel focused. As the new leader, I

talked to each person and sought to understand their aspirations and how they fit in the new customer centric vision.

While on the surface, they were excited to embrace industry practice, they struggled with the transition because it shifted the old way of doing things. Eventually, several team members were unable to make this transition and left the business. Others accelerated through a robust training program using external courses and mentoring. One of those is now one of the top performers focused on driving growth and revenue for the segment they look after. I built a team with core capabilities around field marketing, customer marketing, demand, ABM, and SDR with a view to outsource operational tasks that create less value like running events, creative, and PR while keeping content marketing in-house. These were more easily supported and do not require a certain level of subject matter expertise.

It's also about making tradeoffs and understanding what's going to drive revenue in the long term. For example, while we were focused on driving new business, we neglected the customer. Because of this, in the grip of the pandemic, customer engagement came to the forefront where I was able to create a new competency area to redeploy a team member to drive customer retention and advocacy. There was upskilling and training required - from understanding the fundamentals of CX to specific customer marketing courses. I also used coaching with external marketers that were successful in that role." - Ljubica Radoicic

Concrete Actions:

1. Develop and maintain a skill inventory map based on short-term and long-term plans within the GX framework.
2. Review these every six months to ensure they are still relevant and identify gaps and training needs.

3. Be aware of the environmental factors that require you and team members to gain new necessary skills.

4. Ensure matrix is shared with peer leadership members and C-suite leadership to check that they are aligned and relevant for the direction the business is going.

5. Consult and discuss the training needs with your employees to ensure they understand the bigger picture as well as ensuring the training needs align with their personal development goals.

2. Customer/Market Growth

Returning to our example, the transition from product to solution selling is still a difficult one for many organizations. Sales organizations, at the start, simply do not have the skills or experience to work in this way, and that gap can be a significant source of pushback in adopting new ways of working.

Yet without these new business and industry skills, the organization can't sustainably grow. The team will need to be able to engage the customer around their "pain points" instead of just pushing product features. The team will need to be able to distinguish not only broad business issues, but the specific issues of individual personas, and people.

It is not only Sales and Marketing teams that will need to understand customer pain points and how the solution meets those, but Service teams will too. As solutions offered by the firm get more complex, the expectations around Customer Success will increase as well. Service might begin to look more like professional services/consulting in pre-sales, design, deployment and in Sustain/Service/Continuous Improvement, rather than a "trouble ticket" process.

Further changing up the customer conversation with GX will involve the development or acquisition of new skills.

Relationship skills, for example, are an obvious starting point. Instead of being transactionally focused, teams will need to be able to build trust with prospects and focus accounts over time. The norm might be to mindfully invest time and information in new relationships, perhaps even in areas where the firm can't immediately sell a product so that the relationship is developed for when the customer has a need your firm can address. The Marketing and Sales team will need to be supplemented with facilitation or even entrepreneurial skills if the firm and client will be exploring joint opportunities for growth.

3. People Growth

The people aspect of skills really hits at the heart of GX. How do we create a culture where our people feel that they are learning and growing? Growth is a key driver of purpose for many of us. Without a sense of purpose employees will eventually leave.

Part of the solution to people growth comes from Leadership 101 ideas like delegation, empowerment and stretch assignments or goals. Don't forget the basics.

You as a leader will also need to develop new skills and experience as the Marketing team, and therefore the expectations of the team, grows. In this transition, you'll move from your value being technical skills to your value coming from your ability to lead the team as a rounded leader that interfaces with other functions. You'll have to resist the temptation to try to do everything yourself or micromanage, otherwise you will never be able to fully step up.

The truth is that some of the team might not be able to grow or want to be part of the fast-moving environment often associated with transformation. This, in a sense, is an example of how you can't please everyone all the time. Some will love the stretch and new responsibilities and others will leave. It is about setting clear goals and expectations and sticking with that. Letting some team members strive and others coast is a recipe for disaster. If team standards are continually not met, then the individual will eventually need to be managed through a Performance Improvement Plan.

At the same time, you'll need to see individuals as a whole, not just their job role or title, and look at which elements are flexible from the firm's side. For example, at the time of writing, flexible and remote working are becoming the expectation rather than exception. People are seeking Work Life Balance and meaning in addition to a paycheck.

Key Takeaways:

- Skills assessments don't happen in a vacuum. They must align with strategy and process/RACI. Not all skills are equal or should necessarily be sourced in-house. Commodity skills can often be sourced more effectively by using third parties.

- Attitude is often as important as (if not more than) a particular skill.

- Not everyone will be able to or want to step up to learn new skills.

- Creating a team environment and culture based around openness, growth and incremental innovation is key to having a high performing team.

7
Communications

Communications are like the central nervous system of the body, moving information and feelings around. Sense and response, head and heart. Internal and external communication is not a megaphone for the company to talk about itself and its products. Now more than ever, communication is not a megaphone for *anything*, communication is a two-way street. It is a conversation.

Aren't Marketers great communicators already? What else is there to say?

While Marketers are indeed good communicators with regards to crafting compelling content, the "playing field" of communication is much larger for the Ascending Marketer. This extends both outside the organization to various customer and stakeholder groups, and within the organization at different levels, and across functions.

Communication in multiple senses of the word must be strategic, not only as it relates to the brand, but as it relates to getting work done in an aligned manner to meet growth objectives.

Communication is the story and context that pulls everything together. We have seen several studies that conclude effective communication impacts the bottom line. The *2020 Revenue Generation Maturity Study* concluded that those with above average practice, 77.7% also achieved their revenue goals. The Harris Poll in 2022 shows that *poor* communication costs businesses $1.2 trillion annually.

What's more, we'll not only be communicating about products, services and solutions, or activities, but about business, and even Marketing itself: what we do, and the value we bring to the organization.

A useful mental framework to begin with is AIM (Audience, Intent, Message) as relayed in Russell and Munter's *Guide to Presentations*. We begin our thinking about communications by considering the audience or audiences. Who are they? What do they care about? What do they need?

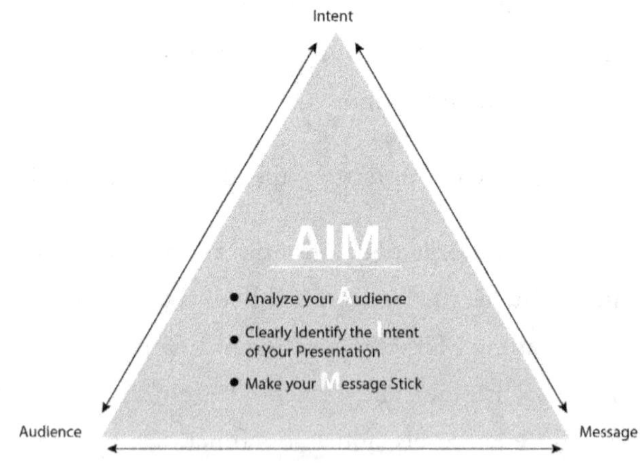

Illustration 11: AIM

Next, we consider what the Intent of the communication: what do we want the audience to think, do or believe as a result of receiving the communication? Then, we think about adapting the content, form and medium of the message so that it achieves the primary intent with the audience(s). Although simple, AIM is a powerful framework to help look at communications in a different way and change them for the better.

For example, plenty of communication with past customers has been about the selling firm itself, and the features of its products and services. If we truly follow AIM, and are honest about our customers, they want to hear about what your products will do for them, how they will help customers to solve their pressing business needs and grow.

Another example of AIM is that as Marketers begin to operate more cross functionally and be increasingly measured in financial metrics, then Marketers must become fluent in the language of business and other functions as well. In fact, being an effective communicator means being able to tailor your personal communication style to what the audience needs, speaking their language by default, rather than your own preferences.

A second mental model for communication is the "plumbing" or "interlock" idea of communication, where you look at how information flows, connecting strategies, plans and processes. How do you harmonize the two-way flow of information, getting to a single source of the truth, and enabling different parts of the organization to "work to the same drumbeat." In practice, what we talked about in the first four chapters is all about operationalizing macro and micro communication.

For example, vision and mission can be powerful sources of communication both internally and externally. Strategy is another powerful communications tool. We must not only decide the content of the strategy, but also the process used to create the strategy in the first place. All the communication in the world won't fix a bad strategy, it also won't fix a strategy that was created without the right contribution from across the organization. This brings us to the best form of communication: participation. More completely, we must consider what roles various stakeholders could and should play in the underlying processes that generate the information in the first place.

First and foremost, when we look at communications within a firm, we're looking at how strategies and plans are aligned, how customer knowledge is consistent and shared, and what ongoing forums exist to keep Sales and Marketing in sync.

Once all these structural aspects of communication are in place, we can begin to look at specific processes and capabilities to understand requirements and the need for tailoring and personalization.

1. Organization Growth

Descending

Most communications are top down and one way. There has rarely been any investment in communications or collaboration tools beyond email. An intranet, if it exists, is mainly a repository for policy and product information and is neither up to date nor complete.

Strategic, business, and functional plans are not standardized and communicated across the organization. In many cases this is because they are not even available in a sharable format and are considered to be on a "need to know" basis.

Communications are seen as a "necessary evil" rather than as a tool to help achieve a range of business objectives and outcomes. Thus, communications tend to be ad-hoc and reactive.

When communication occurs, it tends to be overly formal, "boilerplate," or else technical, and rarely excites or engages customers and employees.

Ascending

Companies at the Leap stage understand the importance of communications and apply different communication methods to effectively engage a range of internal and external stakeholders including their teams, frontline employees, investors, and the media towards desired intents and outcomes.

The leadership team shares all strategic, business, and functional plans with the employees. Team and individual goals are communicated clearly to ensure everyone understands their role in the revenue generation value chain and how they can measure their own success. Personnel at all levels know the elevator pitch to articulate company customer values and often can personalize this with actual examples and stories.

Employees get that "everyone is a salesperson" and are willing and equipped to sell the company and its solutions at an appropriate level.

The company is mindful about how it encourages and invests in informal networks and collaborations such as interest groups. The company has also invested in collaboration software to facilitate these interactions that provide additional synergies, new ideas and improvement alignment over simple email.

The company proactively communicates both good and bad with minimal "spin." There is a culture of open and honest feedback that starts at the top of the organization, but also travels bottom-up and side-to-side through various feedback mechanisms such as Town Halls or 360 feedback assessments.

There is a well-planned and developed external communication system with customers and partners, and the company is geared up to listen to these channels and act on feedback.

In Practice

Good communication begins with all the things we talked about in the first four chapters of this book.

As we alluded to earlier, your first task as an Ascending Marketer will often be to plug into the strategy and business objectives and begin speaking their language!

Strategy is more than a document, it is a way to communicate and align on the firm's focus. By extension, this also informs what the firm is *not* focusing on and what departments should or should not be doing. It is no small thing for a marketer to begin to refer to specific elements of strategy and objectives, it is modeling the new way that Marketing will operate in the organization.

You'll want to map out how strategy and objectives flow down to the functions, particularly to Sales and Marketing, and how the functional plans created within Sales and Marketing map to each other and back to broad objectives.

While this might not seem like communication initially, without this step you'll be in an "apples" and "oranges" situation. You'll be talking about the plan as though it's uniform when there may be two completely different realities. The same applies to focus accounts and go-to-market.

Part of communicating better is having a common vocabulary and consistent definitions to underlie a consistent model of how work is done. As we already discussed, both process and planning are the foundations of an integrated work and information flow. Without being on the same page, communication will be fraught with frustration and misunderstandings. Likewise, communication is easier if teams are working to the same objectives.

This is why we've left the chapter on communication until now. We've already set up many of the foundations of good communication before we dived into this chapter. This includes how structure enables or impedes communication by creating or breaking down silos. A longstanding method of breaking down communication gaps is to have a liaison team member attend or listen in to other team's key meetings or, failing that, to add representatives from other teams to mailing lists, Slack channels, and so on.

This level of integration is particularly important around the core revenue generating processes where you'll want to ensure that information flows and RACIs are completed and optimized.

If you are transforming parts of the organization, training and documentation will be required, including when creating ambassadors or champions for a change. As new employees come on board, they will require a structured onboarding to ensure they get the same messages and information as everyone else. In leading firms, Marketing will often attend the Sales onboarding and vice versa.

Communication also depends on leadership and leadership style. Is information hoarded or shared? Do you proactively engage other peers in different functions, or do you bury your head in the metaphorical sand? Sometimes this might be because you feel that you're just too busy to dedicate time to communication, yet without communication there is often misalignment and wasted effort.

For example, David Grossman reported in "The Cost of Poor Communications" that a survey of 400 companies with 100,000 employees each cited an average loss of $62.4 million per year because of inadequate communication to and between employees.

At a Tech company we've worked with, the President has an open door to team members and cross team visibility and collaboration is encouraged. At the regional level there is a cross-functional working group that looks at growth acceleration strategies, which are owned outside of the individual job descriptions, but various team members collaborate on strategic initiatives to drive growth. That is, whether it is to engage with industry associations; team enablement; addressing key issues, etc. The team meets every Friday to review progress and this committee presents results to broader employees and leadership.

At another tech firm, the leadership team has an open invitation once a month to come and share major operational challenges or roadblocks to getting the job done. Management then looks at how these issues can be priorities or addressed - whether they are specific IT related issues, service, or product.

Collaboration tools such as Slack, and cloud drives have been brought to a head by the pandemic and the move to remote working, but some aspects of "online" communication are better than in-person. Everyone has access to information and can stay informed and contribute their ideas.

In terms of communications "plumbing," mature firms often move to a systematic approach to communications in the form of cross-functional planning processes such as Integrated Business Planning/S&OP. These planning techniques are effectively formalized communication and alignment forums.

Instead of just CC'ing somebody on the product release schedule and calling that communication, there is a regular meeting to discuss that product schedule with various stakeholders in an interactive way. What makes these types of alignment sessions effective is that their whole premise is that decisions will be made and stuck with, based on the information discussed. Any gaps become quickly apparent such as a key launch being moved back, or another doesn't have any marketing support. These sessions are, at best, financialized meaning that the impact to budget and goals is seen, and the information has a rolling horizon. Often interlock type meetings will look 12-18 months into the future, not only to the end of the financial year.

Concrete Actions:

1. Communicate company wide and departmental objectives.

2. Encourage regular team interaction, both up/down and side-to-side in the organization.

3. Form cross-functional teams and adopt project management platforms.

4. Adopt communication tools that have a simple learning curve to optimize adoption.

Before moving on, write down your ideas for the top priority areas where communications must be improved. Are there specific examples where the company has lost money, missed a key deadline, or disappointed a customer because of communication gaps? Have these gaps been resolved? What is the simplest and quickest thing that must be done to improve communication?

2. Customer/Market Growth

The biggest change to customer communication under GX is making the communication two way and into a broader ongoing conversation about growth.

The reality is that in the past customers have spoken to salespeople who've tried to convince them to buy, and then immediately after with a customer service agent to help them with the problem with what they bought. Sometimes the customer has a problem and doesn't reach out to customer service, they just drift away. Not ideal.

CX and concepts such as customer success have smoothed out some of the disjoints here so that the customer is onboarded properly and has all the information and support they need tailored to what stage they're at in the buying and use process. We measure customer lifetime value

(CLV) under CX to show the increase in what we've gotten from the customer over time.

In one sense this is progress, in another it is just one more way of reducing the customer down to a number. We don't love our customers and they know it. The customer is right to ask, "what have you done for me lately?" and "when was the last time you brought me an idea that wasn't about selling one of your products?"

We believe that it is well past time to shift the customer conversation to growth. As we've said before, it is time to make the customer the hero of the story that you are telling and selling. The customer is saying that it is not enough just to be frictionless, tell me the story of the journey you are going to take me on or help me make.

3. People Growth

As a leader, there are three big communication practices to have on your radar that support your growth: commercialization (communication styles), vulnerability, and coaching.

As we've mentioned, the average Marketing leader has been on a journey to talk about marketing activity in financial terms and connect marketing activity with business outcomes. Really this is simply one variation on the topic of understanding different communication styles and the Golden, Platinum, and Titanium rules.

With the traditional focus of business communication around revenue and profit, there is an expectation that business leaders will be at least organizationally bi-lingual meaning they can speak their native functional language as well as the language of revenue and profit.

There is a tendency to treat others as we'd like to be treated, The Golden Rule. In communication styles this means, if you like big picture concepts, speak to others that way even if they prefer numbers.

The platinum rule, common now in business parlance, is treating others as *they'd* like to be treated, communicating with numbers if that's what works for them. In fact, the "them" is often a group, so you'll blend different styles. We've also heard about the "Titanium Rule" which is sometimes a synonym for the Platinum Rule but has also come to mean giving others what they *need* rather than just what they want. Perhaps what leaders need is a composite view of organizational, customer and people outcomes in the context of sustainable growth. GX is a vehicle to speak the new shared language of growth.

It is interesting that we so often look to sports and the military to define what a good leader looks like and how they should communicate. Of late, there has been more talk of vulnerability as an effective management trait and communication style.

Historically, large organizations have been run with a militaristic structure and style, command and control, and even with a degree of fear and intimidation through the "ranks." Tightly guarded information is considered a form of power. Many of these organizations have struggled to adapt and compete because of their structure and communication styles. The hubris and groupthink of "too big to fail" type companies have been well documented.

Thankfully the change in markets has necessitated a more agile organization and with that the expectation that the leader won't always have all the answers. There are more female leaders, and leadership champions like Brené Brown bringing different ideas and styles to the leadership table.

Showing vulnerability can be difficult for anyone as many corporate cultures have penalized vulnerability resulting in detriment to business cohesion, agility, and outcomes. Jim Collins coined his idea of Level 5 Leadership which asserts that it is often the quiet leaders that do a better job than the loud charismatic ones dominating the media and leadership case studies. The established idea of "servant leadership" and the "inverted pyramid" is still a powerful one today. Leaders support their teams rather than the other way around.

For me personally - this is the philosophy I live by and how I lead teams. I've seen putting people first delivers results time and time again. I left one of my jobs because I was expected to bully people and have this kind of directive style. That will take you only so far because people will not trust you. It also creates a culture of mediocre teams. Your team may tick boxes, but they will never go the extra mile and will not go into "battle" with you and for you. This is why it's also important as a leader to be in the "trenches" with your team and work on projects with them. Don't be removed so that you don't know what's happening or what challenges they're facing. For me this is key. Being authentic as an individual, showing that you are vulnerable and don't have all the answers while being a facilitator that guides teams to make the right choices has helped me as a leader. - Ljubica Radoicic

One aspect of communication we haven't talked about is the effect that company and country culture can have on communication and leaders that grow up in those cultures. Perhaps the most well-known study of cultural dimensions is Geert Hofstede's work, which we won't attempt to summarize at any length here but encourage you to follow up on. For example, one of the cultural dimensions is *power distance*, with egalitarianism at the lower end, and hierarchy at the higher end. This is exactly what we just talked about regarding the move from militaristic "high power distance" cultures to the more interactive and flat structures that often help the company be flexible, implement new ideas, and grow.

Key Takeaways:

- The AIM model is a useful framework to not only think about what your customers want and need from your communications but also what your colleagues want as well.

- Although not always first to mind, it is strategy, planning and process interlocks that provide the "plumbing" that operationalizes quality communication throughout the organization.

- There is an important cultural aspect to communications that should be factored in when designing and participating in effective communications.

- Communication makes or breaks companies and teams.

8

Culture

Culture is about how the attitudes, values, norms, and behaviors of individuals at all levels of the organization interact and either positively or negatively affect various financial and other outcomes at the firm.

The outcomes affected by culture cover a wide gamut of the business, including revenue, profit, risk, innovation, growth, customer satisfaction, employee satisfaction, and retention. The Return on Culture study, found that executives who say their culture is extremely healthy are 1.5 times more likely to report revenue growth of more than 15 percent over three years and those with extremely healthy cultures are nearly 2.5 times more likely to report significant stock price increases over three years based on the feedback from public company survey respondents. Our study further validated this as it found that those organizations with better company culture, 78.6% achieved very good revenue results.

Culture is often seen as being set from the top, or as a result of the actions, decisions, and behaviors of leadership over time. As with communications in the last chapter, actions speak louder than words.

Culture is also generated bottom-up, often relating to the nature of core operational work of the business. For example, many B2B firms have an engineering culture, since those firms might have grown out of a distinctive or innovative initial product. The drumbeat of the organization is often around upgrades and product launches. Other layers of culture include national culture, functional, and professional cultures. It is no surprise to hear that the Sales Team and Marketing Teams often have cultural differences in behaviors, values, and norms. These differences are not insurmountable but often need to be bridged through improved communication and shared understanding as well as shared track records of working together successfully.

One of the first steps to improving culture is often building your own and other's awareness that different cultures can exist simultaneously, even within a single individual!

Although people drive culture, the context for culture is also set by the other nine dimensions. For example, by structure or job design, and by incentives and measures. "You get what you inspect, not necessarily what you expect." Siloed structures with unclear roles and responsibilities typically lead to a blame or an "us vs. them" culture that is not conducive to growth. When increasing communication, often a move as basic as relocating teams physically next to each other can begin to create a more positive culture.

We've often seen the case where workshops related to an improvement initiative are the first-time various team members have met in person, which then provides a catalyst for improved working that goes way beyond what is discussed in the room.

The reason why? Transformational workshops often focus on building towards a shared objective and reinforcing what is the same between groups rather than what is different. In other words, shared values. Shared values, such as wanting the company to succeed and grow, provide a challenge to incorrect beliefs and biased perceptions of other teams.

We've seen a surge in the number of organizations recognizing the importance of culture in the past year. Companies want to talk about or "fix" their culture, or to address perceived cultural gaps both overall and between specific teams. The trigger for this is typically some gap in performance and outcomes that the organization is striving for. Perhaps employees are leaving, or there has been some other crisis, or series of crises.

Traditional ways of working are being disrupted. Virtual work and less work travel have allowed individuals to reflect on how well the organizational or industry culture matches up with their own. In toxic cultures, or cases where there is a divergence between organizational and individual values, many individuals are choosing to quit and move on. This is why culture becomes instrumental in the "war for talent."

To make it tangible, creating a culture change should focus on changing *behaviors*.

As part of auditing your current situation, you will seek to understand the behaviors of today that need to be changed because they don't support the business objectives of (today or) tomorrow.

Then working with Sales, Finance, and other functions, you will define new behaviors that do support the new business objectives.

Your intuition is right if you think that these new behaviors must be accompanied by changes in process/RACI, measures and incentives, skills, and the other aspects of the RVC. Culture dictates what *really* happens for all interactions where processes *are not* documented and scripted, and often for what really happens even where processes *are* documented.

We see the idea of GX and building the growth engine as not only a means to an end, but as a commitment to building a culture to do things in a correct and sustainable way. It is imperative to care about your customers and people and a future beyond quarterly numbers.

Developing a positive culture requires work and commitment, and culture doesn't change overnight.

1. Organization Growth

Descending

Organizations at this stage are often characterized by combative or adversarial behaviors focused on individual goals, rather than collaborative ones focused on working towards positive outcomes of all kinds.

Leadership is often "command and control", with little empowerment given to middle management or employees. In the worst cases, the leadership approach can be described as bullying. In other cases, the CEO or other leadership operate as a "cult of personality," focusing on themselves over the organization or customers.

At the team level, a negative culture can lead to a vicious cycle, where employees not only leave but also provide negative feedback on employee review sites and to their network. This makes it hard to hire good people which means problems persist.

There is the belief that all the good ideas are at the top of the organization. Leadership believes that employees are fundamentally lazy and must be kept "in line" and constantly measured and monitored. Being seen in the office or online at all times is seen as a measure of commitment, and maximizing total hours worked is the only way to deliver outcomes. At the same time, poor job performance is often tolerated, so high performing employees begin to think "why try harder?"

There is a large infrastructure dedicated to updating and communicating company policies. When faced with a service situation an employee will quote the company rules that are excessively or blindly slanted to the firm's benefit, rather than to customers or employees.

Innovation is desired in the short term, but failure is severely punished. The organization says that it is interested in customers, people, and making the world a better place, but almost all communication is geared toward complaining that financial results weren't as good as they could have been.

Leadership blames each other and employees. Failures of execution and buck-passing are common. Leaders take sole credit for when things go well, and for their team's and others' ideas.

Sales and Marketing are in their own silos and there is mutual suspicion and blame. Collaboration is rare, and communication or touchpoints are often literally referred to as "throwing something over the wall."

Ascending

Positive culture flows top-down, bottom-up and side-to-side. Leadership should "say what they do, and do what they say" In other words, their behavior should be consistent with their words. The organization's culture is oriented toward making customer and employee lives better, backed up by linking values and mission to strategy, plans, investments, incentives, and key metrics. There is open and honest communication, including when things go wrong.

There is a big focus on the customer with Marketing teams aligning to Customer Success to support engagement and advocacy.

The concept of "win together" is embedded in the organization. Collaboration is not only appreciated but expected to the extent that an "individual win" at the expense of other teams is often penalized and career limiting. The firm has learned to work with and thrive on the creative conflict that often comes with making different teams work together.

Likewise, it is expected that change projects have engagement and input from the right set of stakeholders across the organization, and that these link to strategic objectives.

Meetings tend to be facilitated and interactive working sessions, rather than being presentations or monologues. Questions and feedback are expected and built into the agenda and session timings. "Grandstanding" and "destructive" criticism have been identified as against company culture. People are respectful of each other's time and experience. It is expected that data is woven into presentations and used as an input for key decision making. At the same time, it recognized that it is possible to be both passionate and professional. Stories are used to guide direction and transmit company values and priorities.

Appropriate risk taking and the failures that inevitably go with that are accepted as part of a growth culture. However, teams analyze and learn from past failures, and that these learnings are picked up by other functions and teams.

Leadership does not leave employee engagement to chance. Instead, those at the top conduct engagement surveys more than one time per year, take the results seriously, and act on any items that need addressing. There is a high level of personal ownership role modeled by the leadership team. Leadership takes ownership of resolving problems, rather than blaming employees.

There is generally a culture of continuous improvement in the company that perpetuates without having to instruct employees to do so. Employees and leaders at all levels are empowered to take the initiative and use their judgment when it comes to doing the right thing for customers and people in the organization.

There has been some systematic consideration of work-life balance in the broadest sense and the organization recognizes that it both has a role to play, and it is good business to create a healthy work environment where people can be at their best.

In Practice

The starting point in your current situation might be a Sales team and a Marketing team that seem shades apart in terms of culture. Worse, those cultural gaps are likely materializing into poor revenue performance and resistance to change. This can happen even despite investments in process mapping and leadership that are seeking better alignment and growth.

So how do we tackle these seemingly "invisible" cultural issues, and build a performance culture aligning Sales and Marketing?

The short answer is to focus on behaviors across the teams, to address the contextual factors driving culture, and finally to focus on winning over both *hearts* and *minds*.

Let's look at an example to help explore this further. Perhaps the problem is as broad as plateauing or declining revenues. After some probing from leadership, it is found that Sales and Marketing are essentially heading in different directions.

The solution is to implement revenue marketing, but despite implementing a new program, the pipeline and conversions remain unchanged. After some further investigation it is found that Sales are essentially ignoring Marketing Qualified Leads (MQLs) from the new revenue marketing process.

You might arrive at the conclusion that the process charts weren't clear, or that more training is required, or even better KPIs. Yet, despite tweaking those things, the challenge persists.

At this point we have a concrete example of a negative or undesirable behavior (ignoring leads), even though the new process and RACI charts say Sales should act on them.

We know what the desirable behavior is as well. So, how do we change the behavior from the undesirable one, to the desired one? Although people generally want to do the right thing, simply telling a person or team to do something is rarely the way to sustainably change behaviors.

Instead, we need to dig into the reason for the behavior and analyze both the individual's underlying reasoning and beliefs, and the broader factors affecting culture which go hand in hand.

In terms of contextual factors, we're talking about the alignment of things like strategy, customer focus, planning/budgeting/incentives, process and RACI clarity, structural alignment, skills, communications, technology, etc.

In other words, have we configured the 10 components in a way that supports the desired behavior, or in a way that contradicts it?

Often, we expect people to perform a process against what that same person's incentives suggest. People *rarely* do something that contradicts how they are measured and paid. This is particularly true when there are no consequences for *not* following the new process, and if the new behavior doesn't match the "pulse" of the old ways of working.

An illustrative example from B2C is the change we've seen to the process of purchasing cars. The customer has "changed" since they now arrive at the dealership fully informed about pricing and options, having done their homework online. While the "hard sell" might have been somewhat effective in the past, it can have the opposite effect today, driving customers away. Yet walk into a dealership today and there will still be rows of shiny-shoed blokes (inevitably) ready to pump fists and talk sports. Somewhere in the back of the room is a soft-spoken individual handling a growing number of "internet inquiries" with those inquiries driven by overarching branding and the website (a parallel to digital transformation effects in B2B). Several services offer to shortcut the physical dealership altogether!

Although this is a B2C example, it can also clearly apply to B2B, the purchasing rhythm and expectations increasingly being driven by the buyer, rather than the selling firm.

The other path of analysis is to look at how individual and team beliefs and values affect behavior. All other things being equal, team culture and momentum favors optimizing for that team rather than optimizing for the organization. Often, given organizational silos, the trust between different functions is also low by default, leading to a view that other departments must fend for themselves.

In the case of our example, an individual might know that there is a general expectation that they should act on MQLs, but when push comes to shove, they fall back on what has always worked such as going back to the same old accounts rather than looking to new leads.

The solution to this issue must start with leadership on all sides committing to make a change, often through a recognition that *not* changing is not an option. But leadership support alone is not a magic wand for cultural change. That support enables the program to overcome its teething troubles and deliver an experience of joint "success." It is invoking the power of shared values around "winning together," backed up by the actual experience of winning that will change culture over time.

When planning a change, you should first seek to understand what's important to the functional teams involved and try to bring beliefs and assumptions about the "rules of the game" to the surface.

You will need to find a shared objective, value, or existential threat bigger than a single team to bring them together.

In the context of shaping organizational culture around customer centricity, Marketing has a critical role to play as the custodian of the overall customer experience and "voice of the customer."

Hence a Marketing leader in organizations that are truly customer-centric vs. product or sales first, has a bigger role to play influencing functions like HR, Customer Success, and other customer facing functions. Having led both Marketing and Customer Success teams, I have found that the key to creating and driving a customer centric culture lies in orchestrating cross functional teams around joint vision for the customer and the brand promise.

By creating and optimizing customer engagement frameworks, forming a CX baseline and journey maps that align teams, we were able to embed a truly unified vision and clear goals and metrics. This had a profound impact on customer growth, retention, and loyalty. - Ljubica Radoicic

To change culture, start by looking at behaviors.

Concrete Actions:

- Clarify and communicate values, discuss with your functional team members what these values mean to them so they can be translated into day-to-day behaviors.
- Reinforce positive behavior. The positive behavior of employees should be reinforced by leadership in a manner that motivates employees to work more productively thereby increasing their self-esteem and confidence.

- Encourage open communication as it builds trust and creates a healthy workplace atmosphere, so areas of improvement are not seen as criticism or blame. Even getting rid of the managerial offices can make a huge impact on cultural change.

2. Customer/Market Growth

CX is a recent incarnation of the ongoing drive towards a customer centric culture.

In a sense this CX (and digital transformation) reorientation is one borne out of crisis rather than planning. Firms had to adapt to their customers increasingly moving online. That move has left firms with a virtual treasure trove of new data, and still looking for ways to use that data.

We see an opportunity to use that data as the basis of a new culture of exploration and conversation with customers where it's now possible to hone in on growth opportunities at an individual level.

Data could redefine the possibilities of what customer success means and build an entrepreneurial culture focused on supporting the customer's growth.

Is it possible that having an entrepreneurial culture, rather than a transactional one, sometimes means helping the customer win even if it doesn't directly lead to a sale at that moment?

This is one of the behavioral changes that we talked about in the last section. To understand the potential of GX take some time to listen in to and observe customer touchpoints across the different channels of your firm.

Based on the behaviors you see, how many of these touchpoints are currently treated as transactional, or even act to shut down growth ideas? How should those behaviors change to open the growth conversation?

You might take your observations here and form them into a pilot program where the firm changes the "script" on how customer interaction will flow, and let it gravitate towards growth.

Using the RVC is a way to attune yourself to the day-to-day happenings within the organization that otherwise might have become invisible. You learn to see again, as if you are an organizational detective, scientist, or anthropologist!

You can simply ask "does that behavior support growth" as you go through a day in the office or during online meetings. You can ask yourself these questions in relation to your own behaviors or about your team or others You can ask the question about interactions with the customer. Using a lens of growth lets you see specific opportunities to productively change behaviors that you wouldn't have otherwise seen.

The point is not to assign blame for what others are doing "wrong" but to build a story that contrasts the way things are today, and how they can be in future.

3. People Growth

The place to start with people growth is to look at your own leadership style. Do you really foster a risk-taking, growth centric, entrepreneurial culture or do you tend to close down left-field ideas that might prove valuable? Part of this might even be subconscious resistance to the "new" due to you being overworked. Do you make space for new ideas to emerge?

At minimum you can be an advocate for the customer. You can help lead the organization on the journey of adopting an experimental approach to exploring new ideas.

Getting the right culture really comes down to the soft skills and example of leaders. This is where articulating values and defining them in practical ways is extremely important. Values on paper are useless unless they are turned into behaviors that uphold those values. Time is allocated to allow teams and individuals to reflect on what those company values mean to them in their roles and how they relate with each other in the team and with customers.

When I was managing large teams, I made sure that I articulated the values and behaviors we want to exemplify and created those channels of communication to foster an open and honest environment. Failure is not looked down on but seen as a lesson for us to learn from. Success is celebrated but shared across the team as no one can succeed without all team members functioning in alignment. Lead by example, always! When employees see their leaders behave in the same way that is expected of employees, those employees feel inspired! - Eve Chen

For me when hiring a team, I don't like people who only want to tick boxes and be there '9-5'. It's a challenge to build the right mix of people on the team. I'm conscious that not all can have that passion but it's important from a team culture perspective.

I had interesting feedback from one of my team members who, when asked "what do you think about the team and how things are going under Ljubica's leadership?" said that they were tapped on the shoulder to return to their previous employer but wanted to remain in their current role.

They were learning a lot and there was significant growth potential. So, it's important to create a culture of innovation, progress, and challenging the status quo. It gives people the opportunity to challenge themselves and grow. This again brings up GX and connects culture with the skills conversation. - Ljubica Radoicic

Key Takeaways:

- Culture is built from a pattern of actions, decisions, norms, and behaviors over time. It sets the context for positive or negative results because the culture is a powerful force affecting individual and team behaviors in the real world.

- A way to improve Sales and Marketing alignment is to look for shared values and a way to "win together." Identifying an existential threat to the company can be a powerful force to bring the company together based on commonalities rather than differences. Scanning the external environment and talking to customers may help surface these types of threats that might have always existed but were effectively "invisible" prior.

- Building a growth culture means allowing measured risk and rewarding risk taking in this context, even if it sometimes results in failure. This is instead of only rewarding success and always punishing failure, which tends to reinforce traditional ways of working, and stifles innovation.

9

Analytics & Reporting

"Given our mission, how is our performance going to be defined?"

Joan Magretta and Nan Stone, Harvard Business Review

According to a recent study by MicroStrategy, companies worldwide are using data to:

- Boost process and cost efficiency (60%)
- Drive strategy and change (57%)
- Monitor and improve financial performance (52%)

In fact, research by McKinsey shows organizations that invest in big data yield a six percent average increase in profits, which jumps to nine percent for investments spanning five years.

Our study also indicated that of those organizations with better practice in this area, 81.3% achieved their revenue goals.

Throughout this book, we've talked about the importance of fostering a fact-and-data based culture if the company is going to grow. To support that culture, we need "the right measures, measured right." Yet often the underlying data is inconsistent, or we are simply no longer focusing on the right things.

While base financial measures such as sales/revenue have largely stayed the same, digital transformation has changed underlying processes and roles and responsibilities for generating those sales. This is why we need to start looking at new and different underlying measures if we want to be able to pull the right levers to affect revenue.

Artificial Intelligence has meant that firms are able to understand buyer behavior in a more sophisticated way which brings predictability into performance and helps us understand how specific activities or messages influence behavior.

At the same time while we're able to understand the buyer at increasing levels of detail, we're often still unable to understand some fundamentals of our own business, for example, around detailed customer and product profitability. If Sales and Marketing are to work together to drive revenue, we should use all the information on hand to provide insights on the most profitable customer and product combinations.

Costs, including supply chain and overheads, are lumped into large buckets rather than matched and attributed to individual customers and products. Once these costs can be properly tracked and allocated it is often found that some customers and products are fundamentally unprofitable. They may be cross subsidized by other customers and products. We are adding to revenue but destroying profit.

Sometimes this is because of previously "invisible" aspects of the Sales process that become clear when interviewing the Sales team or doing process mapping. For example, perhaps the Sales team doesn't have the right materials or message to convince potential customers to sign, so they "give away the farm," including free shipping, support, or other favorable terms to get the prospect across the line. By working together to "debug" this situation it might be clear that the prospect/customer has other unmet needs that are more valuable than free shipping. Meeting these needs can turn an unprofitable relationship into a profitable and longer lasting one.

Of course, this is not all for Marketing to work out and certainly not in isolation. However, we can foresee that while the focus is on revenue generation and simple ROI today, trends such as demand shaping, and cost-to-serve will inevitably mean that businesses will look to become even more focused and integrated tomorrow. That is, on generating and sustaining business with the most profitable customers and based on the most profitable offerings.

This revenue versus profit question is not a new one, particularly as it applies to growth, and won't be resolved soon. In the meantime, Marketing and the organization have a lot of work to do around measuring and getting insights from the GX concept of orbits. That is, how do we get sustainable revenue and growth from making Customer Acquisition, Retention, and Expansion a virtuous cycle? And then what does that look like at the process measure and forecasts level, so that we can collect process efficiency and effectiveness data that helps us anticipate revenue and make course corrections as necessary?

Those are the questions we intend to give perspective on in this chapter.

1. Organization Growth

Descending

There is little focus on analytics since attention is on scrambling to get all the work done, i.e., no "plan, do, review," just "do, do, DO!"

Where KPIs do exist, they are superficial and based on whatever is easily trackable such as leads or MQLs, rather than what (process) moves the needle on macro business outcomes such as revenue. The mindset is that Marketing only owns the top of the funnel leads and is not responsible for the full funnel.

There has been little effort to develop standard definitions for KPIs. The same measure might be calculated differently depending on the system, function, or business unit. Underlying data has rarely been cleansed or harmonized.

Decision makers rely on perceptions, past decisions, non-validated be-liefs, and anecdotal evidence. There are no defined data management or analytic processes to support insight development or business decisions. There is little or no postoperative review, as by then the organization has moved on to the next crisis. There is a proliferation of roles whose tasks are to manually generate and reconcile custom reports, rather than gen-erate insight.

There are few deep analytical skills or executive interest in building a data driven culture. Projects and activities are all done slightly differently so apples-with-apples performance comparison and sharing of learnings becomes difficult or impossible.

Ascending

Companies at this level have a strong data and analytics culture. Both Marketing and company-wide leadership are constantly looking to squeeze new insights from existing data using advanced analytics looking both forward to the future as well as backwards.

There is a clear understanding of which processes and levers drive business results. Typically, the core revenue generating processes of Customer Acquisition, Retention, and Expansion have already been mapped and integrated. Measures exist to show process "health" and allow course correction. Forward looking metrics provide a predictable view of future revenue.

There is a standardized data process deployed company-wide to support specific insights which are "financialized" to show their impact on financial goals. There is a continuous improvement cycle in place to refine processes, enhance data, and optimize resources/automation of data collection and insight generation. Report generation is automated. Data definitions and sources have been harmonized, greatly reducing the need for reconciliation.

Leading practices are shared across the organization. The "plan, do, review" process is embedded, and data management and specification of projects is standardized to allow information sharing across the company.

A data driven organization is one that has established a framework and culture where data is prized and effectively used to make decisions across an organization - from Marketing, Sales, Finance, Product Development to Human Resources.

At a financial services firm, my client was using a lot of traditional marketing mixes to promote their services such as direct mailing, TV ads, as well as telemarketing. The company has been operating for 10 years with mediocre revenue growth results. They knew that they had to adopt digital marketing tactics as the world was rapidly moving towards digital channels and consumers wouldn't even talk to a company like theirs until they did all their research online.

As part of the exercise of developing Persona profiles, I analyzed 10 years' worth of customer data they had in house. We first sat down with each functional leader and set the relevant KPIs including profitability, sales velocity, revenue, and revenue growth and started to group customers based on these metrics before building out the demographics, sociographic, behavioral as well as psychographic profiles for these personas.

We made sure we reviewed against the new data we collect every 3 months to ensure the accuracy of the profiles we crafted to allow us to make informed decisions to deploy effective campaigns with accurate targeting for the outcomes we want

As a result of convincing the leadership team to adopt such a data centric practice in looking at their customers, we increased qualified leads by 44%, reduced cost per lead by $186/lead and improved sales productivity by 12% as well within 12 months.

My team then developed relevant dashboards in the system we built for them and with each functional leader having real time access to dashboards with metrics relevant to their functions. This successfully built a data centric culture in this organization, and they grew to position #284 in Inc. 500's fastest growth company in the country as a result. - Eve Chen

In Practice

Ask, "how will we measure (the business impact of) that?"

These few words can help launch a transformation of how the organization decides, analyses, and measures what it does.

If Marketing is still early in its measurement journey, then this question will signal to others in the team that the culture is shifting from activity focused, to business and outcomes focused.

Often, we use a driver tree type diagram, like the example below, to help link processes and outcomes.

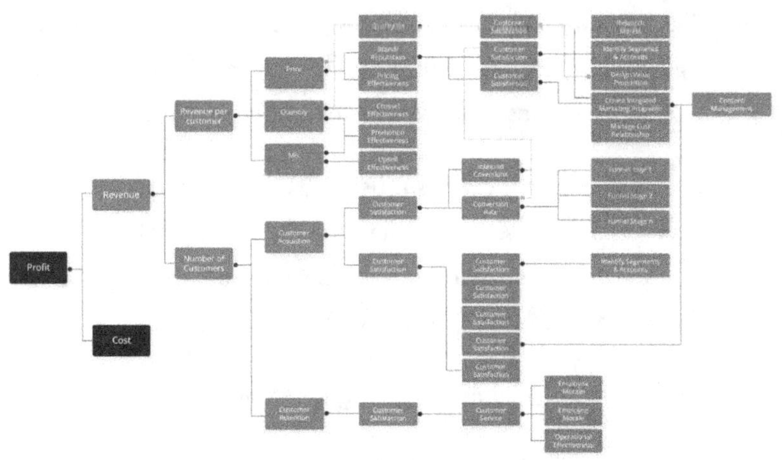

Illustration 12: Value Driver Tree

Using a value driver tree can help the Marketing team (and the organization) align over how marketing and business activities connect with revenue. It becomes quickly apparent when existing measures do not seem to connect with key outcomes at all!

As a starting point, you should be able to draw a diagram like the one above and talk through the connecting arrows. Each box is a driver or lever affecting one or more boxes on the left of it. For example, quality and brand both affect price. Exactly how they affect price, and how to move those levers effectively is what the organization will need to work out.

At this stage, there is no arrow between customer service and price, but even today, good service might allow a slightly higher price to be charged, and service might be the difference between getting a new customer and not.

You will work through the drivers and levers so that they paint a useful picture that helps drive decisions. Although "everything is connected to everything," we suggest you only draw the biggest impact arrows between boxes, representing what really moves the needle for results.

Next, some metrics and measures must be associated with these arrows. In your business, if you use Marketing Qualified Leads (MQL) and Sales Accepted Leads (SAL), what are the typical numbers by time period, and what is the typical ratio between the two?

What does a good range look like in those metrics?

Often organizations will color code the metrics with a traffic light (Red, Yellow, Green) or similar method to highlight whether the metrics are inside or outside of expected ranges.

We're naturally skeptical when we see a KPI report that is all green particularly if the organization is struggling with overall results. Often this indicates that either the right metrics are not being measured, not being measured accurately, or the ranges are not set correctly.

For example, most people think that anything above ~80% is good, perhaps recalling school testing ranges, that's still an "A-" in some places, right! If we're talking about successful new innovations, then 80% would be stellar. But if we're talking about the number of airplanes that make it to their destination without crashing, then 80% means we're not buying a ticket, no matter how cheap!

Once a relationship between metrics has been established, your team will be able to troubleshoot or debug what the numbers are indicating. Continuing the example from above, Sales Accepted Leads may often be significantly lower than MQLs. Rather than simply accept that as a fact of life, the next step will be to work with the Sales team to diagnose what the reason behind that might be.

The need to periodically adjust metrics ranges is a natural part of transformation, and a desirable outcome from ongoing continuous improvement.

For example, when you start running, a 9-minute mile is average, and 8 minutes might be good. As you get fitter, 8 or 7 minutes might be the norm and 6 minutes "great." Eventually, you'll begin to benchmark yourself against the world's best time (under 4 minutes, approximately 3:43 currently, in case you like a lunchtime challenge).

Unlike running races, numerical benchmarks for Marketing performance in your firm versus others won't always offer an "apples to apples" comparison. This is due to differences in business structure, process execution, and other areas. These benchmarks might provide useful directional information. For example, if you respond to customer website inquiries within a week and the standard for your competitors is one day then you probably still have significant room for improvement, regardless of any small differences in structure.

What is often more comparable across firms are the principles and practices associated with good performance, which we've distilled into the book as "ascending" practices as well as part of the various frameworks and suggestions we've shared.

Many businesses have created metrics for acquisition activities but are not as focused on metrics for customer retention, expansion, and CX metrics overall. So, the next step will be to build out *those* metrics in your driver tree.

We've talked about output and outcome metrics. Another type of metrics are process excellence measures, and these are often associated with compliance or error rates and service level agreements. For example, Marketing might agree with Sales that the Sales team will review all new leads within a certain time period. As a different example, the organization might want to instigate a post-meeting review for the customer presentation team after each in person meeting with the prospect.

You'll need a holistic set of measures at the executive level that cover the elements of GX and financial measures, plus the detailed measures and reports that feed those at the functional level. Teams should be able to drill-down on summary metrics to understand the "whys" in the underlying data at various levels of abstraction.

As the saying goes "data is the new currency" and unfortunately in this digital age, a lot of organizations struggle with metrics and reporting because of an overall lack of investment in data governance, strategy, and a long-term technology roadmap.

This in turn impacts the various cross functional teams that rely on data and business intelligence more broadly for decision making. The irony is that usually these organizations are the ones who are trying to sell digital transformation, data standardization and profitability to their customers, yet they themselves are not able to achieve this internally.

From my experience having worked in several organizations that faced this challenge. The result is misalignment and no one trusting the data! - Ljubica Radoicic

Concrete Actions:

- Identify analytical needs in organizations. Determine where the deficiencies are by surveying or assessing employees to determine their analytic strengths by segment.

- Build analytical strengths by training necessary employees in analytical abilities, increasing analytical skills with strategic hiring, and importing abilities from other areas of the business.

- Identify deficiencies in technology for processing large data streams and by making sure that your enterprise-wide systems can store the amount of data needed. It needs to be easily retrievable, and can collect and protect all data, keeping even data not usable with today's capabilities available for future use.

- Embrace the analytical decision-making mindset as a Marketing leader, get used to justifying to your peer management using data and analytic insights (this will gain you a ton of respect especially among CEOs/CFOs, & COOs.)

2. Customer/Market Growth

As we've stated, you'd be hard pressed to find a company that isn't focused on the customer and has at least a baseline set of customer metrics. However, we often find that these are weighted to customer acquisition and lighter on customer retention and customer expansion.

Taking customer acquisition as an example, the firm will also need to consider how to measure the acquisition of *new* customers or bookings from *outside* the traditional focus segments and markets. The KPIs for new industries or markets e.g., conversion rate, might be adjusted downward in the short term to account for the learning curve associated with doing something new.

Many organizations are already looking at Customer Lifetime Value to develop a playbook for how to make a single purchaser a repeat or multi product/service purchaser. This comes back to the cycle of Customer Acquisition, Retention, and Expansion under GX that we talked about at the start of the book. We like the idea of an orbit rather than trying to "trap" a customer in a funnel, infinite loop, or whatever. The customer is free to leave any time, but we hope that they'll choose to stay because they love us. So, that begs the question: how do you measure the power of love?

At the risk of our attempt to inject a little joy into this section falling flat, *how do we measure* the sum of rational and emotional calculus that causes one customer to stay and others to leave? What is the status of this gravitational pull at any time? How do we measure how effectively we're supporting the customer and helping them grow? Like any relationship we need to ensure that we're not getting complacent, we need to monitor the signals and, ultimately, ask them.

Often a firm will want to measure % of revenue from new products. Perhaps in the future under GX the firm will try to measure the value they've added to their customers over time more holistically.

It is common for professional services firms, for example, to measure the total benefits delivered to a client, and the total amount invested through "free" projects. They then use those numbers to market to the client in different business units, countries, as well as to other clients to accelerate sales.

These firms are also continually looking for ways to move their fees from hourly rates to outcome (aka value) based pricing.

For example, a services firm might typically estimate a client project at $50,000 based on the hours taken to do the project. However, from experience the firm might also know that such a project will almost certainly generate $500,000 in benefits for the client. Taking a value/outcomes-based approach the firm decides to charge the client $150,000. This, in principle, is still a win-win.

There are endless variations on this scenario, the firm can charge $25,000 guaranteed down payment but get a total of $250,000 if benefits are delivered as expected.

This is not an exhaustive coverage of the topic, and certainly not suggesting that this is right for your organization's situation, in business you must always perform your own assessment of likely risk and reward.

Taking a newly entrepreneurial approach to customers has risks, and the firm must have the right people and capabilities in place. While we've already said that everyone in an organization should be able to sell the firm and its values and generally be on the lookout for opportunities, what we're talking about here is beginning to adopt a systematically more entrepreneurial approach for some roles and in some parts of the organization.

We provide this as a counter example to the "usual" approach to increasing revenue and profitability i.e., get more customers at any cost! Instead, think about optimizing the pricing based on a better articulation of value to the customer, and finding the right audience for that message, such as more senior execs, who can listen to and act on that information.

Rather than advocating throwing caution to the wind, we are encouraging you to shift your idea of "trapping" a customer in the funnel and getting the initial sale into exploring what the customer really wants and needs, and how you might be able to work together to get a much better win-win.

There is a clear opportunity for firms wanting to implement GX concepts to invest some time working with customers and clients to not only ensure that products and services are adopted and used but to provide a methodology to calculate the benefits of the firm's solution, and even help the client measure those benefits using real numbers. You can pilot different growth approaches with real customers, and jointly agree the goals and measures for that activity.

While working as the Head of Marketing for a workflow solution company, I was introduced to the concept of "Customer for Life." The concept was brought to life through a set of clear, mutually agreed behavior and performance indicators created for teams and individuals in the organization that align with customers' performance indicators.

Our consulting team worked with customers in seven target industries to develop mutual goals and success metrics. These metrics were then translated into departmental and individual metrics within our organization to ensure the right actions were taken to support the achievement of customers' success as we had defined it.

A five-year Value Journey program was then developed to measure and track the success over the contractual term with customers. The program provided the customers with clear milestones and expected ROI and financial outcomes are also clearly defined by milestones.

Every quarter, our customer success managers initiated progress reviews with these customers against those mutually agreed success metrics. The result for the organization was a 97% achievement of its Customer for Life goals and the organization was able to win many look-alike enterprise customers and dominate these seven industries by presenting to customers not only the target outcomes but also the methodology that would be used to achieve this success for our customers. - Eve Chen

3. People Growth

As we've alluded to already, part of the growth journey in Marketing will be to get comfortable developing and using financial metrics in interactions with the rest of the firm. For you, the leader, this will involve getting comfortable being measured on revenue, and ensuring that you have the right sets of data, KPIs, and reports to track towards achieving those targets.

The next question, of course, is how do we measure the success of GX from a people perspective?

There are gross measures such as number of training hours delivered, and employee engagement and retention scores. Firms are also increasingly using culture surveys to try to better understand the strengths and challenges in the culture. These surveys often look at whether a company or department is living its values.

A related idea is the use of 360-degree feedback for leaders. If appropriate, you might also seek to get direct feedback from your peers in Sales and Finance, not only on the Marketing team, but on you as a leader.

Finally, it follows that if you will be piloting a process of working with customers on co-developing growth initiatives, you will also look to try to measure people growth on both sides of the "fence."

There is no doubt that it feels good to really add measurable value to clients. This also helps establish a track record, and thus also for moving roles and organizations. It is also often good for morale for typically non-customer facing personnel to work directly with customers and be part of something new.

Working on realizing the potential of GX is a development opportunity for you and for various teams in the organization. In addition to macro surveys of employee metrics, you should debrief any GX pilot sessions as well as record anecdotal/qualitative measures of how things went.

Key Takeaways:

- Despite the linkage of increased customer knowledge to increased conversion/revenue, there hasn't always been a uniform growth in the understanding of customer and product profitability. The journey to implement GX orbits will eventually include a business case or detailed metrics around customer and product profitability and the economic benefits to profits of retaining and expanding relationships with customers.

- Be wary of trying to measure too much too soon. Start with fewer but more insightful metrics that enable discussion and decision making, then extend from there.
- Metric development and benchmarks go hand in hand with understanding strategic questions such as what constitutes value, and what are the different ways value can be created and delivered to both customers and to employees.

10
Technology

"When digital transformation is done right, it's like a caterpillar turning into a butterfly, but when done wrong, all you have is a really fast caterpillar."

George Westerman, MIT Sloan Initiative on the Digital Economy

Rain trickling down green leaves, splashing on paving stones. The percussionist drumming drip drip drip. Gray day. Green. Growing. Growth. Automatic. Rivulets on window panes. Quiet. Silence. The worms are having a field day. Thrum, Thrum, Thrum. Sound. The space you needed to grow. Go. Coming. Becoming. Trees, grounded and flowing.

After starting this book with a story about how technology is transforming marketing, we've intentionally left the detailed discussion on technology until now. The reason is that everything we've learned over the past decades means we've come "full circle" back to where we started.

That is, we have been reminded again and again of the need to get everyone else in the organization working together to best benefit from that technology.

We've developed the RVC as a paradigm, checklist, ready reckoner to look at change and technology in a holistic way. Using that approach will help increase the likelihood of success in your change initiatives, and over time you'll have created the building blocks that allow your firm to make change and core capabilities that support growth in good times and bad.

Developing your Revenue Generation Value Chain allows you to exploit the potential of new technologies as they emerge, rather than constantly playing catch up. We're excited to see how technology will further enable the marketers of today and tomorrow.

In this chapter, we'll talk about how the Martech "stack" acts as an enabler for organizational growth, how CRM, ABM, and AI support go-to-market and campaign management, and how the CMO can no longer be "hands off" with technology.

According to McKinsey's report on uncovering the connection between digital maturity and financial performance, it's clear that mature companies enjoy a range of benefits that go beyond improving bottom line. They see benefits such as improved product quality and customer satisfaction that contribute to better financial performance. Other benefits include environmental sustainability, increased workforce diversity and broader social responsibility. The report talks about seven pivots, the notables are: data mastery, intelligent workflows, unified customer experience and business model adaptability. All of which provide sustainable growth and competitive advantage.

Another study from BCG looked at more than 180 publicly listed companies from around the world, finding that digitally mature organizations outperformed their less mature competitors across all financial measures.

The *2020 Revenue Generation Maturity Study* further validated that the more mature organizations are with their technological applications, the better they are at achieving their revenue goals.

1. Organization Growth

Descending

Organizations at this stage might still be trying to ignore or resist Digital Transformation. Many Sales and Marketing customer engagement processes are still manual. The website is a list of product brochures, and contact details, sometimes even just pointing the visitor to the company's switchboard number.

Where marketing technologies do exist, they are usually based around using automated email to contact customers. There is no overall technology roadmap, and business functions are left free to find and implement solutions that they can carve out the budget for.

Customer information exists in multiple systems and there is little or no integration between systems, or a single source of truth. There is little or no governance over business architecture or data. Critical customer information might sit on systems that are no longer supported or have insufficient security protections risking brand and reputational issues. The Sales team, and other teams, do not use CRM as a mandate.

Technology is often seen as a necessary evil and treated in terms of minimizing costs.

Ascending

There is an established technology architecture and roadmap extending out at least the next 3-5 years. The CIO role exists and is actively involved in looking for technology that can enhance processes and deliver business value and growth. This can either be to streamline and improve productivity or above-the-line benefits to improve customer engagement.

There is a well-defined Martech strategy that's aligned to the buyer journey and overall customer lifecycle. The CIO works with functional leadership to ensure that the organization is not constantly chasing the latest "shiny toys" without properly integrating and getting the benefit of existing technology.

Data and systems are under formal governance. There exists a single view of the customer, and data and systems are integrated, providing quality data to power dashboards and KPIs for real time decision making. There is a formal security protocol to protect customer and company data and prevent breaches. The company considers the principles of ethical marketing with respect to technology, over and above the minimum standards set by legislation.

The firm has an established project management office and/or methodology to help ensure that implementation projects are deployed in a structured way, and learnings are shared across the organization. There is a formal training program to ensure that users get the most out of core systems.

In Practice

The truth is that rarely does a technology ecosystem grow in a totally structured way. It's more likely that technology will evolve in an organic, semi ad-hoc way based on the whims and desires of previous groups of leaders.

You might have inherited a situation where the organization has already invested in a system that few are using. In that case part of your roadmap might include first remedying the current situation to provide a solid foundation before investing in more advanced capabilities.

We're suspicious (and you should be) of any technology audit whose only recommendation is to invest in an expensive new technology to fix all the problems of today, without exactly specifying how.

Instead of looking for the technological silver bullet, you'll work with IT (and even Sales, Customer Success, and Finance) to develop a roadmap across the other nine elements of the growth engine. You'll also develop an accompanying prioritized list of technology and non-technology fixes.

You'll look at your Martech stack and work through the abundance of options and offerings to find what works best for your needs, including how well the new tech will integrate with what you've already got in place. Not surprisingly, more and more of the marketing budget is allocated to technology.

Exactly what is in the Martech stack will differ depending on several factors, but it typically includes the following layers:

- Customer Relationship Management

- Content Management System
- Web Analytics
- Brand Analytics
- Marketing Automation
- Account Based Marketing
- Social Media Marketing
- Search Engine Optimization
- Live Chat and Survey Tools
- Paid Advertising Optimization
- Business Intelligence

In addition to the above the organization's Enterprise Resource Planning (ERP) system should be kept in mind as this is often the master for product and financial data. Because of this Marketing will need to understand how to reconcile between revenue attribution in other systems, and revenue numbers in the ERP.

We've seen slides discussing the Martech stack for individual organizations with 25-60 system names on there, and it is estimated that there are now close to at least 10,000 Martech system options. It is easy to get caught in the loop of constantly looking to add the newest and best technology without properly bedding down and integrating previous system investments. It is not unusual (and we fear it is the norm) that organizations use only a fraction of the functionality of the system they've invested in, and only a small percentage of users use the system. It might make sense to look for a less powerful and complex system that users will use rather than paying high fees for something they don't.

A measure of the effectiveness of technology is how well it enables core revenue generating processes within the organization.

"The Game Plan" is the priority input to developing the technology roadmap. The top-line, revenue/customer, and resource strategies should be mapped out. Processes and metrics should also be identified first so a full scope of the technological requirements can be made, including the tools needed to support the deployment of customer-facing programs and backend tracking and reporting. From there the right technologies can be identified to support those activities. - Eve Chen

This is one area I've seen companies and Marketing teams struggle with - when there is no clear ownership of Martech strategy and technology roadmap. It leaves the door open for various teams within Marketing to reactively solve problems by building tech stacks that are disconnected with poor adoption and governance.

The result is increased cost in resources, greater internal silos, and disconnected data. A great way to overcome this is by creating centers of excellence that feed into the overall Martech strategy. These centers are collaborative in nature and take into consideration current and future needs.

A clear example of how one tech / SaaS company tackled this challenge was by implementing a hub and spoke model. The Marketing operations team owns the overall Martech strategy and deploys it, supporting global programs. On the other hand, regional Marketing teams are treated as satellites, meaning that specific capabilities and technologies are deployed locally based on strategy, needs/market fit, and skills.

E.g., As part of optimizing lead conversion, the regional demand generation team had a need to deploy a tool that would help accelerate sales conversations. Hence, a chat bot / AI tool was implemented that was part of the existing global tech stack.

This approach gave the regional team more flexibility to deploy tools as and when needed, as well as maintain overall integrity of Martech strategy, data, and governance. The regions were empowered to inform the overall Martech roadmap and leverage best practice when needed. - Ljubica Radoicic

We can then use the decision driver tool to map out the type of technologies required to digitize data and transform them into intelligence for business decision making. It is critical to involve IT partners in the organization to leverage their knowledge and other IT-related compliance requirements such as cybersecurity, overall IT strategies and governance. ICT, media, finance, and professional services have been very advanced in adopting digital transformation, but revenue generation organizations seem to be lagging in best practices to adopt digital transformation.

Even digital body language is focused on a silo of marketing practice without overall growth or GX in mind. If we can develop the relevant metrics for each element of GX, a business will be in a better position to develop its digital transformation strategy over the entire revenue generation lifecycle. If you take digital transformation over the asset lifecycle, there are a ton of digital initiatives and strategies to be found, but there is hardly anything out there documenting a holistic approach to the revenue generation lifecycle. More work needs to be done in this area!

Concrete Actions:

- Conduct a review of your current technology vs. the strategy and processes that technology supports to form a clear understanding of (any) benefits. Technology for the sake of technology can create more issues.

- Consider putting in place a data governance strategy and create a steering committee to break down silos.
- Apply the concept of "incremental innovation" to test and digitize specific processes before committing to bigger technology investments.

2. Customer/Market Growth

Technology plays a key role because it can provide GXO leaders with data and insights for a more holistic view of the customer lifecycle from first touch to churn or retain and thus empower them to engage in a more meaningful way. Technology underpins this strategy. It also supports the overall digital transformation of customer engagement and experience.

The starting point for many organizations looking to enhance customer understanding will be to better integrate customer data across several back-end platforms, including CRM, to provide a more comprehensive and accurate view of the customer. This integration already represents a significant amount of work, even before getting to designing and implementing the newer and more sophisticated tools.

Bear in mind, it is already *not* a given that teams will use the designated systems correctly or at all. For example, your Sales team might not be using the CRM.

The need for better integration and systems compliance may have already been picked up if you're in the middle of a CX initiative. Better integration of back-end systems should provide you with both improved visibility of the prospect or customer across channels while also making the customer's experience more seamless as well.

At the time of writing, many of you will already be working on an Account Based Marketing initiative in one form or another. As we've mentioned, you can start your ABM initiative without new technology by working with sales in a structured way to coordinate accounts and people lists that match your ideal customer profile.

Adding Artificial Intelligence (AI) and automation to ABM allows you to jointly target a broader range of focus accounts. This means not just dream accounts but other target accounts, and even more that might not have been on the list but are still signaling that they are in the market to buy.

ABM provides a solid foundation for GX because it allows the Sales and Marketing teams to think about the specific needs of individual accounts while also adding multiple levels of detail to personas. On the other side of the coin, we've seen businesses use some ABM tools as the entirety of their ABM strategy which turns into another ad spamming machine. True ABM cannot happen without well-defined and aligned Sales and Marketing strategy which may or may not involve ABM tools and technology. The effectiveness of ABM technology can also vary dramatically between macro geographic regions, for example it might work well for North America, but it may not be appropriate in the Asia Pacific region due to fragmentation of markets and different languages.

Over and above ABM, AI might provide the firepower for firms to compile opportunity analyses tailored to individual customers on the fly. These analyses could then provide the basis of growth conversations, adding value to the customers own view of their competitive positioning and industry opportunities.

Next, we'd have to consider what the technological enablement of GX might look like, the GX orbit being a cycle of Customer Acquisition, Retention, and Expansion that helps us and customers to grow.

One thing is clear, that we'll want to begin to measure, track and analyze new/different things. With the funnel now morphed into an "orbit" under GX, we'll want to start tracking different types of conversation rates or "stage gates."

For example, we'd be interested in (new) reports or analysis that let us answer the following questions:

- Which makes a one-time purchaser (customer) into a repeat purchaser (client)?
- What characteristics of customers indicate that they are more open to discussions of further purchases or different products and services from us?
- What moments of truth indicate that the customer might leave? This is not just poor service, but the lifetime of the existing deal or product is nearing the end, or the market has changed, and we need to re-pitch our customer to make them a client.

Although these types of questions might already be asked or thought about today, what we're looking at to enable the GX orbit is an integrated view of customer and client health, opportunity, and growth. What are the critical success factors, measures, and enablers for consistently turning "suspects" into clients for life? And how do we reliably get our clients to bring future clients into our orbit?

3. People Growth

As we've discussed throughout this book, digital transformation has been the broad arc of technology changing how B2B buyers operate and thus what Sales and Marketing need to look like to capitalize on those continuing changes.

This technology enabled journey has also been a personal journey since the nature of Marketing jobs has evolved. There have been many obstacles to overcome to even get this far. Martech has allowed the more routine tasks in marketing to be automated or outsourced.

Some aspects of this new technological literacy are mundane in a sense such as being a better stakeholder and functional representative for back-end integration projects to unify data sources and create a single view of the customer.

It might have been tempting in the past for marketers to be hands-off with these types of infrastructure projects, leaving them to IT. The challenge is that although not "sexy," these projects consume time and expenses and lay the building blocks for future tech-enabled capabilities.

If those projects run over or head in the wrong direction then there may not be the budget, resources, or "slots" for future development. Quite simply, Marketing needs to be engaged and well-informed enough to advocate for itself for IT alignment.

This idea of a well-informed technologist also applies to the ability to translate business requirements and capabilities into what is required from technology and vice versa. It's the ability to deal with and manage third party tech firms and service providers

Given new responsibilities and budgets, the Marketing team itself is seen as a potential customer of other organizations trying to sell Martech solutions. It will pay to know the right questions to ask when engaging with vendors and trying to separate hype from reality. Caveat emptor (buyer beware) absolutely applies to finding the right solution and solution provider.

The internal and stakeholder engagement aspects of technology selection must also be managed. We've often seen cases where a CMO selects a Martech solution without engaging their teams and that solution is not adopted. As a leader, you'll need to bring your team and the organization along on your technology transformation journey. More of that in Part Two.

Key Takeaways:

- The best solution to a problem might not be new technology right away. Look at the 10 components holistically and seek to build alignment ahead of new investments in technology.
- Technology investments should clearly demonstrate that they seek to improve and optimize revenue generating processes, rather than work at odds with them.
- Marketers are increasingly becoming technologists. It is no longer possible to be hands-off and only a consumer of IT.

* * *

Before moving on, take the time to jot down the answers to the following three questions:

- What are your main takeaways from Part One?

- Which single idea was the most powerful for you?
- What is the single greatest challenge you see for you and your organization to implement the ideas in the book?

If you scored each of the 10 areas using the 1 to 5 scale or traffic lights, which areas stood out as having the highest potential value i.e., the biggest problem or opportunity areas?

How would you explain to a friendly colleague what is going on in your organization now, and the opportunities for the future organization? Is the GROW model useful to help articulate this story?

What will happen if the organization doesn't act on the problems/opportunities that you see?

How about applying GROW to your own career and situation. What might the immediate future look like for you? What will you need to have conversations about? What will you need to stop talking about? What things need to be in place for you to be successful? Which people can you help, or can help you move forward on the path to growth?

PART 2

Transforming the Organization

"Dream, Plan, Reach"

Michael Phelps, American former competitive
swimmer & Olympic gold medalist

*"It was a few minutes before the hour. Which hour was it again? Still early
on a Tuesday morning. I tried to rub the bed-at-1am sleep out of my eyes
and work out what I was going to say in the next meeting. My calendar
already looked like the angry blinking screen of an air traffic controller at
Sydney's Kingsford Smith Airport during rush hour. Don't people check my
calendar before putting new meetings over an existing one?*

*So many planes to land safely today. Planes that had been mid-flight even
before I'd started this job. And yet I'd earned a reputation as somewhat of
an expert in rebuilding planes in flight. That is why they hired me. Lucky
me!*

*I thought about this book. Got to bring it back to the real stuff – Sales and
Marketing and Revenue Generation, and you. Who am I to advise you on*

what to do, anyway? And yet I'll try. That damn imposter syndrome and immigrant work ethic!

It is important for me to pass this knowledge on. To give something back for the opportunities I've had. It is not just about working harder than the next person, but about the truth and doing what is right. It is about working out how we can all win together.

My screen clicks on, and it is my co-authors. It turns out that we are all outsiders (and as it turns out, immigrants). Outsiders making this book happen when none of us have the time, only the drive to help others and move the conversation forward. Two of us now live and work in the US, although we've popped up in every type of city around the world to get the job done: London, New York, Hong Kong, Paris, Cape Town, Manila, Mumbai, Brisbane. You name it.

A strong vision, humility, and the will to push through apply everywhere you can and will go. Sometimes it is all we have to begin with, and we have to make the rest up as we go along. Perhaps you have more. Perhaps you have charisma and political aplomb and even a head start. If so, then go confidently, but stay humble. As Ascending Leaders, we want the results, not the limelight. Stepping up will sometimes take all that you have and all that you are to be a true leader. And for that, we're here for you." - Ljubica Radoicic

How do you feel after reading Part One? Energized, overwhelmed, a bit of both?

Can you imagine presenting Growth Experience (GX) and the Revenue Generation Value Chain (RVC)/Growth Engine to your firm? Why or why not?

If you feel a bit overwhelmed, then in Part Two you'll see the practical aspects of how you will use GX and RVC in Marketing to create a growth strategy or transformational project.

We'll describe the Ascending Growth Method (AGM) structured approach to change, which is designed to help you frame and implement your new project or strategy.

To support the practical application of the materials, we'll also share a real-world case study, based around AGM, and discuss our learnings from applying the AGM approach.

The benefits of using a structured approach to change are that it improves the certainty of outcomes and that it reduces the project and implementation costs of misalignment. And finally, a structured approach to change includes the right level of governance to manage organizational, people, and customer risks of change.

As we said in Part One, building sustainable growth is not a "one shot" exercise. The organization (and you) will need to develop the capability to manage change through ongoing phases and cycles of change while building on continuous improvement.

Making change that leads to growth is the "superpower" that you'll develop by putting the ideas in this book into practice. That's the big story of this book, empowering you and giving you the freedom to move up in your career and life, to make a positive change in the world.

Effecting change is not a spectator sport, in fact it can be one of the most challenging and rewarding things you can do in your career. It can be fun too. Although not stress free, having the right tools in your toolbox can give you the confidence to help lead the organization to work differently, and work better. That shared experience of tackling a challenge with people from different parts of the organization forges memories and relationships that last a lifetime.

Given the cyclical nature of growth challenges, our AGM approach to change is also cyclical.

Here, again, is a picture of the AGM model for change and transformation:

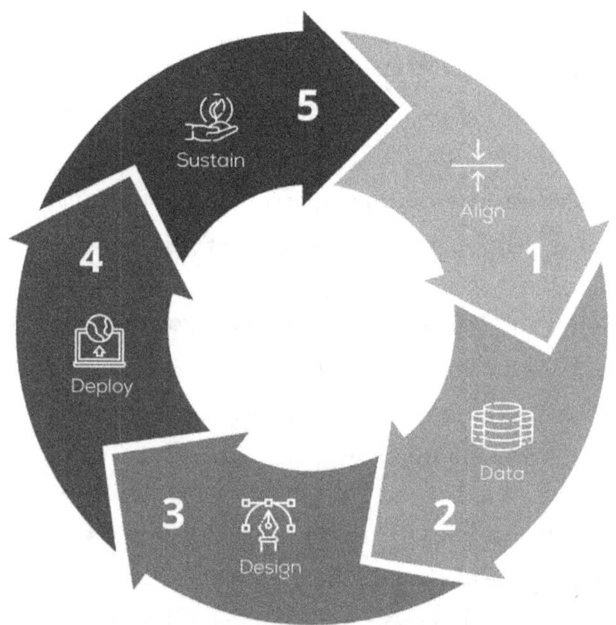

Illustration 4: Ascending Growth Method (AGM)

The stages of AGM are:

- Align – understanding and lining up expectations of what is to be achieved, context, as well as the approach and what will be required from team/leadership.

- Data – gathering and analyzing foundational data to identify key underlying issues, understand potential opportunities, and build the detailed case for change.

- Design – developing the blueprint for change across the ten dimensions of the RVC model (i.e., increasing maturity and closing the performance gap).

- Deploy – putting changes into practice to upgrade capability and performance in Sales and Marketing, as well as across the organization.

- Sustain – transitioning improvement projects to business as usual so that improvements "stick" and benefits are realized. This is all about continuous improvement.

The approach is not only important so that you and your team stay organized and don't miss steps in managing the change, but also so that you can guide the rest of the organization through the change process.

The amount of time each stage takes depends on the complexity and scope of what's being tackled, but these stages remain the same and are done in sequential order although some iterations between design and deployment may happen.

The next five chapters cover AGM in detail. The best way to use Part Two of the book is to apply the material to your own situation as you read through.

If you took notes or scored each of the 10 areas of RVC in Part One, then that information will feed into your walkthrough of AGM in Part Two.

While you will be familiar with storytelling in the context of your organization's products and services, there is also a need to tell stories about you, your team, and the journey that the organization will take as part of implementing a growth strategy. Often, we forget this, assuming that everybody knows what Marketing does and the value they bring. In many cases the organization might have a legitimately poor view of how Marketing has operated in the past, and thus part of your work as an Ascending Marketer is to build trust, and to turn that perception around.

We recommend you practice creating and refining your story of "why change?", what that change might look like and, if required, what is different this time from other attempts to make a change in the past. You might even practice saying this out loud! Often telling this story (e.g., elevator pitch) helps get your own thinking straight, and helps to assimilate the learnings from this book.

Make notes on the chapters in Part Two with reference to the situation at your organization. What is your personal context for this new strategy or project? What is the trigger or inciting event that has disrupted the status quo for your organization? Why change?

Remember that AGM is a gap closure approach, just like GROW that you heard about in the first part of the book.

In fact, AGM maps roughly to GROW as follows:

- Align maps to "G" Goal setting i.e., setting the vision and expectations for the strategy or transformation program.

- Data maps to "R" the Reality of your current situation. Data proving the underlying problems and opportunities.

- Design maps to "O" the Options for future Design that will solve the problems of today, and create strategic capabilities that will power growth over the next 3-5 years

- Deployment maps to "W," the actions that Will need to be taken to put the new design into practice.

- Sustain tasks can be added to "W" in the previous stage or added to GROW so that it becomes GROWS.

One premise of this book is that implementing a challenging transformation strategy program can change you professionally and personally as well. You will grow as a leader, but what does that mean?

What are the characteristics that you associate with good leadership? Think about it for a second before reading on and make a note of your thoughts. Can you imagine in your mind's eye what a good leader looks or sounds like? Can you imagine what you might look and feel like, stepping up to be an even better leader than today?

You might have a view on what makes a good leader but there are many ideas on what makes a good leader, some of which might appear contradictory: visionary, thorough, sets direction, empathetic, pragmatic, vulnerable, strong, open minded, focused, inspirational, a good communicator, ethical, courageous, acts with integrity, develops others, and so on.

The point is that you will need to develop a leadership style that is authentic to you, and get results, based on a mix of the above traits as you work on transforming growth. Best to start with the end in mind, recognizing the need for growth, and be open to change and development of your leadership style.

Undertaking organizational and personal change at the same time can be a lot to take on, so it helps if you have a mentor, coach, or even consultant to use as a sounding board. This helps keep your development process "honest" in terms of giving you objective guidance. We've created the Ascending Growth podcast and community to provide additional sources of information and inspiration in this area!

At a minimum, why not do a quick leadership audit of yourself. Based on Part One and the visualization you just did, what is your Goal for your skills and abilities as a leader? What is the Reality of where you are today? What is the single most important leadership development area that you will work on?

Let's start!

11
Align

"Just as your car runs more smoothly and requires less energy to go faster and farther when the wheels are in perfect alignment, you perform better when your thoughts, feelings, emotions, goals and values are in balance."

Brian Tracy. Motivational speaker

It is often a mistake to jump straight into solution mode without "preparing the ground first."

During the Align stage, part of that preparation involves discussing and aligning expectations about your role and the new strategy, project, or opportunity that will transform the organization. You are seeking input and commitment from key stakeholders around the planned change or new strategy.

This alignment usually takes the form of a series of conversations with leadership and other functions about the *why, what, and how* of the proposed change or new strategy.

Although you might have been recruited into the organization or promoted into this role to "make change" it is still necessary to align stakeholders on what this change really means in more detail. People want to be part of the action, rather than having an action done to them. Having alignment with leadership from the start is a critical factor in your success. This starts with getting others to buy-in and contribute to the overall "story" of change.

Next, the organization will need to feel confident that you have a process and a plan for making the change or bringing the new strategy to life. Often, you will develop a "90-day plan" which is a way of organizing and communicating what needs to be done in the Align stage and beyond. Importantly, the plan also provides the basis of your expectations of what you need to be successful, such as access to key personnel and information, and visible leadership support for the new initiative.

In addition to being a tool to support transformational change, the Ascending Growth Method can be used to support ongoing strategy development and implementation as part of business as usual.

In the Align stage for a transformational change, such as the move from product to solution selling, you'll be working on establishing both the vision and *case for change*. Both are part of this overarching story that helps the organization contextualize, understand, and assign meaning to the change.

The *vision for change* includes articulating the "big idea(s)" behind the vision for the future of Marketing and the organization as a whole.

That unifying idea might be as simple as "growth" or "the need to change to survive and grow," or whatever your organization has in its growth strategy. It might be a drive towards customer centricity. It might be diversification of the market and customer base. It might be Growth Experience (GX) and/or The Growth Engine.

Part of the vision for change will inevitably be fixing the issues of today but, given that change takes time, the vision must also include building a future-fit organization by looking three or more years down the road. The vision for change must describe a desirable and compelling vision of the future that is markedly different from today. Otherwise, why change?

The case for change is a story that describes the benefits and drivers of change. It answers the "why?" of the situation as well as the "why now?" and why doing nothing is not an option. Perhaps the organization has plateaued or fallen behind competitors. Perhaps its key markets are in decline, and it needs to revitalize its customer base. Or maybe margins have declined, and the organization needs to find a way to increase the size and profitability of new sales.

Sometimes the vision and case for change will be combined into a single document, presentation, or story. Each of these must still be individually compelling to inform the organization both "where" (vision and direction) and "why" (case for change).

One without the other won't create forward momentum for change. Both the vision and case for change should be written into slides with supporting information that will be further defined and detailed in the Data stage of AGM.

The vision and case for change will also be part of the elevator pitch you'll use to engage your peers and leadership in meetings and through formal communications. Therefore, you must consistently be practicing and refining your communication style so that you can tailor this message to various audiences. By doing so, you're able to create variations of the story that closely meet the needs of Sales, Finance, Leadership, and more.

Despite the advantages of developing the vision and case for change collaboratively, you should still expect to meet some level of resistance when trying to work this way, if it is different from the usual ways of working today. People tend to defend the status quo, even if it isn't working particularly well.

The type of seismic shift that an idea like customer centricity represents often brings out the worst in people before it brings out the best. Individuals fear for their livelihoods and place in the pecking order.

People fear what they don't understand, and sometimes they simply don't want to put in the effort to understand. Better to find this out and try to deal with it proactively at the start!

The formal process of managing alignment is called "stakeholder management and communications." You'll build a list of all the people or groups who can influence the success of your strategy or are impacted materially by it. Whether you're new to the role or have been around for a while, the stakeholder management process enables rigor and focus, particularly since people move or move on, and different stakeholders will be affected differently by different types of changes.

For each stakeholder or group of stakeholders, you will first gauge their perception of your leadership and the project (e.g., using traffic lights), and secondly, estimate the amount of influence they have in the success of the project.

The results take the form of a 2 x 2 matrix. On one axis, perception is plotted from low to high, and influence is plotted on the second axis. The estimates of perception and influence are calculated based on initial conversations about the project or strategy or based on reported remarks from other stakeholders. You can even simply ask, "who supports this initiative, who is likely to oppose it?"

Then, focusing first on low perception, high impact pairings, you'll devise a plan of how to address those stakeholders through different forms of communication, meetings, workshops to move those stakeholders in a positive direction.

Having some key stakeholders ranked "red" or "low" isn't necessarily bad for the project, it is just reality. Time and time again the biggest opponents at the start of an initiative or new strategy can become the biggest supporters by the end.

Objections often contain at least a legitimate grain of truth, and sometimes represent new perspectives that uncover "blind spots" for the project team or for the new strategy that you're developing.

When first working cross-functionally, you can't know what you don't know about how other functions outside of Marketing work. A positive response to an objection is often to start a conversation and to allow the objector to share their view of the situation.

You'll continue to refine the overall story of the new strategy with input from others, and it will become a joint story that is meaningful to everyone in the end.

So much of the work an Ascending Marketer will need to do now and, in the future, will be working across traditional roles. You'll need to blend creativity, structure, coaching, analytics, and political sensibilities with traditional marketing skills. And frankly, you'll need some grit too.

Typical Activities in the Align Stage

Let's give you a quick look and feel of the types of work that happen during Align.

Typical activities include:

- Aligning the objectives and "what success looks like" for what you're planning to do with leadership, other functions, etc.
- Understanding the context relevant to your plans in terms of triggers or business needs, history of other projects, related strategies or plans, other projects, and so on.
- Being aware of the scope, timelines, budget, etc.
- Having insight into known problems related to your strategy.
- Building a list of people that you should speak to or involve in your strategy, developing agendas for those meetings, and scheduling the appropriate in person or virtual meetings.
- Articulating and iterating the vision for change and case for change.

After an initial set of alignment conversations, when the problems are clear and there is consensus around the need to do some work in the area, you'll begin to do some activities to plan for the work ahead.

These detailed planning activities include:

- Building a master list of documents and presentations that you need to review and requesting these from your team.

- Generating a preliminary list of where expected issues or opportunities might be based on the ascending and descending practices you read about in Part One. Having an idea of what problems will be fixed and the benefits of fixing them.

- Creating a plan for the other data you'll need to get to conduct your project and which forms, forums, workshops, data extractions, interviews, surveys, and so on.

- Documenting scope, timeline, budget, and seeking formal approval to conduct the project (if applicable).

In the past, we've used a 90-day plan to organize our work and to communicate with the organization. The plan can be in the form of slides and will document the overall objectives and goals for what you seek to achieve and describe the key activities and milestones during that period. The time to implement different types of initiatives using AGM varies. But as a rule of thumb 4-6 weeks duration is a reasonable timeline, for a person new in role, to complete an audit including Align and Data stages, and to develop initial recommendations as part of the Design stage, while also tending to other onboarding and other business as usual tasks.

This equates to roughly half of the 90 days. The remainder of the time can be allocated to piloting and implementing the new initiatives such that at the end of 90 days there has been demonstrable progress against objectives. You will use the information in this chapter and next ones to identify the activities that go into your 90-day plan.

In Practice

The AGM approach helps avoid the tendency we have as marketers to jump right in and start trying to find a solution before talking to anyone else.

Prior to meeting others, it makes sense to do some pre-work to get your ideas and supporting data points down on a page as a starting point for discussion.

We have often used a "one pager" document that consists of a diagram and bullet points about the topic to help frame a discussion. For this document you can use GX, RVC, or AGM if applicable.

Even if you don't use the page, it is handy to have it in your back pocket and pull it out if any conversation is getting off track. A parallel benefit of this preparation is that it helps you to rehearse the story of your vision as well as anticipate likely questions or objections.

Two questions that you should prepare to answer are "What's in it for me?" and "What do you need from me?" Being blindsided by these simple questions may undermine your credibility!

Alignment discussions can be "selling" as much as "telling." Given that most organizations already have too many projects going on, you will want to ensure your case for adding another is clear. You want to demonstrate an inclusive, collaborative way of working, while still respecting that others might have limited time to give to your project.

As Ljubica is fond of asking "how can we win together?" Alignment emerges from finding shared victories and recognizing that the only way the organization can win is to do so together.

Don't forget that it will be necessary to seek and monitor alignment within your own team. Some of the team might initially fear change, or not want to step up at all.

If you will be conducting an improvement initiative in the form of a project, we recommend that the project team compile all of the relevant factors like scope, timeline, and resources into a formal Project Charter document. After this, you should get the document signed off by relevant stakeholders *before* diving into the next stages of AGM.

At times, priorities or the situation will change, and you'll want to have documentation to "remind" everyone of the agreement. Even if you don't do this in a project charter, you'll need to outline the approach for your project or strategy, including a detailed timeline for the next stage, Data.

While you might have introduced "big ideas" during the Align stage, the Data stage is where you'll gather the evidence to back up the vision and case for change at a detailed level.

You will conduct data gathering and analysis through interviews, data/KPI extracts, process mapping, workshops, and other methods. Getting all this information sometimes has a lead time, so it often makes sense to request this information during the Align stage.

You also need to estimate the time it will take the different teams to complete the Data stage. Leaders in other functions might fear that your fact-finding will monopolize their team's time while there is still a business to run.

Be mindful and document your interactions with other teams. Get an agreement up front and time in the calendar to minimize surprises and help to prevent delays due to scheduling conflicts.

If you're still looking for ideas on where to start, below are some further prompts.

Concrete Actions:

Here are several concrete actions that you can get started with in the Align phase:

- Review business strategy and Sales planning documents and use this to plan how you'll align the work of Marketing to the overall strategy.
- Dig through available data to find facts and develop a story that suggests the need for improvement in processes and performance.
- Review this list of typical and detailed activities presented earlier in the chapter.
- Develop a 90-day plan as appropriate.
- Develop a data gathering approach that articulates what you'd need for the organization to prove or disprove your hypotheses and to gauge the scale of the problem/opportunity.
- Begin to develop and test your story of the growth journey in terms of current context and issues, improvement areas and approach, and benefits of change.

Next, we'll introduce a case study to give you a look and feel of approaching a marketing transformation in the real world, and to illustrate the discussion in this chapter.

Our case study looks at a newly hired external resource coming into the Marketing lead role. They are tasked with transitioning the organization from product to solution selling.

Remember that although the case study will raise certain issues and situations from an illustration perspective, when completing the exercises to apply the theory you will be thinking about *your own* organization (or a previous one that you know well).

Even if you are already in the middle of a project or new strategy that isn't using AGM, you might find things that were missed, or new ideas that can be incorporated at your organization. It is not too late to bring those ideas to the table now if it helps increase the likelihood of success of the new project/strategy. This is particularly the case around getting the right stakeholders aligned with the project, it's never too late. In this sense you can use the AGM process itself as an audit tool to assess current and recent projects and find both opportunities for improvement and note things that you did well (even if not in AGM) that you'd like to make sure that you do again next time.

Case Study

The organization is a global provider of specialist enterprise software and solutions, servicing a broad range of verticals. Its core markets, including the industrial and resources sectors, were stagnating due to several macroeconomic factors, negatively impacting long term revenue prospects for the organization. The organization has a market leading position and is constantly under threat from new point solutions entering the different markets.

A newly hired Head of Marketing is appointed to lead the marketing team and navigate changing business priorities in challenging times. The Marketing leader is responsible for the go-to-market strategy and programs these teams deliver.

The key business goal is to drive growth by diversifying into new markets, enabling the company to stem revenue declines, and hit a growth target. Leadership recognizes that Marketing isn't where it needs to be to meet the new strategy, with the marketing team operating in a transactional and reactive way. Leadership trusts that you, the new Head of Marketing, have the structured process and experience to remedy the situation. That is why you've been hired.

Case Study - Applying the Theory

Your objective is to develop a plan for the first two weeks of the Align stage as it applies to your organization. Go back to the chapter content and create a short list of 5-10 bullets of what you'll do, and who you plan to speak to in terms of roles. What types of questions will you ask? How will you articulate the story of the change to the business?

Case Study - Align Stage Outcomes

In the real study, the Head of Marketing created a 90-day plan and secured buy-in from senior leadership on the approach for the 90 days, and for providing support and making staff available for meetings. Then the new marketing leader set out to meet key stakeholders in Marketing, Sales, Product, Services, Operations, and Finance.

In meetings with stakeholders, the marketing leader began with questions such as:

1.   Tell me about your role? Who are your main stakeholders?
2.   How do you work with Marketing?
3.   What's working well?
4.   What's not working well?
5.   What are your key priorities for this role/team/organization?
6.   If you could change one thing, what would that be?
7.   Why?

The initial conversations also provided the opportunity to learn details of the go-to-market structure, and to begin to form relationships and initial alliances with other leaders in the organization. Despite generally positive engagement, there was also some push back from some stakeholders around "why change?"

The marketing leader began to create a mandate for change by showcasing the value of Marketing as a growth and revenue driver. This was done by applying best practice B2B sales and marketing strategies, including the benefits of moving from product to solution selling.

Case Study - Discussion

Despite the approach being close to textbook, there was still pushback from key personnel. This is to be expected and represents what we call a "moment of truth" that sometimes can make or break a new project or strategy. If the marketing leader wasn't prepared, having a grasp of the story and case for change, and asking the right type questions, then they might not have gotten permission to proceed on to the Data stage.

Importantly, the Marketing leader listened and wasn't defensive as the stakeholders gave their perspectives on what was working well with Marketing and what wasn't. Of course, this is easier to do if you've been hired externally. Even if you are already within the organization or role, it is still important to ask these questions in the context of the new growth strategy or objective. An important part of becoming a better leader is to develop the humility to seek and listen to feedback, and to recognize that no one function has all the answers, including Marketing. You will demonstrate through your words and actions, particularly in these initial meetings, working to help the organization "win together."

Lastly, make further notes on how you'll approach the Align stage at your organization.

Chapter Conclusion

Transforming the organization is as much about leadership, alignment, and approach as it is about developing brilliant ideas and technical solutions.

Alignment is an ongoing process rather than a single meeting or memo. The crux of alignment lies in fitting Marketing's efforts into the broader business context, aligning expectations and the touchpoints with other functions, particularly with Sales, Finance, and the Leadership team.

As a business leader, you'll start from where you are. It is not a sign of weakness to ask questions. Also recognize that you'll need to market yourself, the marketing team, and the new strategy using both your words, and your actions.

12

Data

The Data stage is about building the informational foundation for future stages of the strategy or project. This is done through gathering and analyzing quantitative and qualitative data, interviews, review of documents, workshops, and so on.

Although there may be a general idea of the weaknesses in the organization, there is often a lack of consensus on exactly what the real problems are, or how to solve them. Trying to build a future on this type of foundation inevitably results in failure because while you might end up fixing a lot of problems, they may not be the right ones.

If the Align stage was about establishing the vision or "Goal" in the GROW model then Data is about building a fact base on the current "R," Reality. Finding the gap between where you are and where you want to be is the key to identifying exactly what needs to be addressed.

The Data stage takes the form of an audit or maturity review of the current status quo. The functional scope varies but will almost always include Sales and Marketing and Customer Service, plus aspects of Finance and IT. Looking at Marketing in isolation will not enable you to build an integrated, growth centric organization as the pieces of the "engine" will not fit together well.

During this stage it is critical to understand:

- Business performance
- Scorecards
- Sales model and compensation
- Sales performance
- Key marketing metrics/KPIs
- Pipeline metrics, Product, Customer trends
- ROI

Depending on the organizational structure, interviewing functions such as HR, Engineering, Product Development, and others might also be part of Data gathering, if they directly impact how Marketing performs its work.

This collaborative approach is a change from the way that most organizations look at themselves. The focus is often on each function optimizing itself and hiring the kinds of leaders that can make that functional optimization happen rather than the expectation being to work or optimize across functions.

In reality, all of the core revenue generating processes that you'll map in the Data stage *are cross-functional,* and thus require an "end-to-end" approach to document, analyze, and optimize them. This end-to-end approach follows the real buyer journey from start to finish, or from start to virtuous cycle in the case of GX. There is an analytical focus on handoffs and roles and responsibilities along the way, rather than only looking at a piece that one silo performs.

There is often the question of "why waste time studying what's happening today. We know it's broken, let's just move on to designing the future?"

The truth is that similar to a mechanic or doctor, you want to do some testing to be sure that you've found the real problem.

It is not until you get beyond the symptoms of the problem that you can reveal the real "root cause."

You solve the root cause, and the symptoms go away for good, whereas only tackling the symptoms means that problems will reoccur, and you'll be stuck in a cycle of firefighting. It's helpful to explain to other leaders why the data gathering and analysis approach that you are suggesting allows enough time to be clear on the real root of the issue before moving on to solution mode.

Just like a doctor might use an x-ray, you will build pictures of the business through data analysis and process mapping. You will be able to point to your picture and say "look, that's where it is broken."

When the root causes are laid bare, the real problem and way forward become clear. The organization moves from treading water to swimming forward.

You will be able to put the impact of what is broken into business and financial terms. You will be able to answer, "why change?" and "why change now?" with concrete facts.

For example, if the organization has a low win rate on new client pitches because they don't have the right skills or materials, then the cost of those losses can and should be calculated and aggregated to support the case for change.

You will also be able to tell what is working well and potentially even what currently differentiates you in the customer's eyes. Almost never is an organization doing everything wrong. You'll gain more credibility by acknowledging a bit of what is working well, while balancing this message with reinforcing the need to change!

Making a case for change is important as the initial enthusiasm for a project or new strategy wanes when the amount of work needed dawns on participants. Unless the team can spell out "why change?" in black and white, the initiative might be stopped dead in its tracks before it has even really begun.

Typical Activities

Given that the objective of the Data stage is to have a fact and analysis base to support your strategy, typical activities include:

- Gathering data through workshops, interviews, data extracts, document analysis, surveys, voice of the customer, etc.
- Mapping revenue generating processes
- Analyzing data, diagnosing key issues, identifying opportunities

- Developing a preliminary business case and roadmap for the strategy or initiative(s)
- Presenting findings to leadership and gaining approval to move forward to Design stage

In Practice

The Data stage often takes the form of an audit of the current situation with respect to the vision and requirements for the future, while looking at specific functions and cross-department relationships.

Some examples of the data you'll look at:

- The GTM strategy, business plans, and performance
- Sales data - Sales account strategy/set up, Sales plans, reports, etc.
- Customer & CRM data - segmentation, personas, top customers, customer spend, churn, customer satisfaction, etc.
- Marketing performance - marketing effectiveness and efficiency review (channel performance, pipeline, etc.)
- Customer success info - product adoption, CSAT, NPS, churn, report reviews
- Specific focus on database and data quality
- Operations review (Sales and Marketing ops)
- Understanding of all processes that underpin the buyer journey and customer experience

The discussions you had with other personnel in the Align stage are likely to have been brief and focused on getting buy-in for potential future strategy. Now you'll want to go back and formally interview relevant leadership and others about the strategy or project you're working through.

Use the ten areas of the RVC as a checklist for what you'll cover in the audit or review. Under each one, identify initial questions and the people you want to speak with. The numerical order of the RVC provides a logical sequence for your review, so begin with Strategy (1) and work through to Technology (10).

The reason to do things in this order is twofold. Firstly, the earlier ones influence later ones.

Secondly, it helps you avoid wasting time on problems that don't have a material impact on business objectives.

After some preliminary analysis of Strategy, Customer, and Planning you will need to look at revenue generating processes in more detail.

You will already have some theoretical knowledge of segmentation, personas, and journey maps when you analyze the current state of Customer Knowledge. Next you will seek to understand how this really works in practice and how these things intersect with Customer Acquisition, Retention, and Expansion.

Your organization might already have some of the Customer Acquisition process mapped out, especially if it has already started working on CX in a substantive way. However, the reality is that though these processes are rarely complete, legible, or even accessible. For example, unless your organization has a formal and well-maintained process repository, any process maps relevant to marketing might end up in a folder on someone's desk in IT.

Plan on spending time with "doers" in Sales, Marketing, and Service in a working session to map out an overview of the Customer Acquisition, Retention, and Expansion processes. These don't need to be at high levels of detail, instead focus on drawing a picture for each process in 1-2 pages that shows the basic flow, handoffs, and current issues. It's also helpful to have an overview diagram that shows how the existing processes do or do not fit together in the current state.

This can usually be completed in a 1-2 day session, depending on what other chunks of work you'd like to include in the working session.

While the joint teams are in the room, you can also explain some of your vision of the future and get them to prioritize the most relevant issues and opportunities by providing supporting examples.

You may even want to split the session so that one day focuses on the current state of things, and the next session discusses opportunities driven by customer centricity or GX. Although the next stage of the approach is a formal design phase, it often makes sense to get ideas from the team to help illustrate potential fixes to current issues and the benefits of more integrated ways of working.

Make a point to write down both quality examples and direct *quotes* from working sessions and interviews you conduct. These quotes and examples are mini stories that do the work of influencing others and building the case for change.

Often when the authors capture quotes to build the case for change, we don't attribute them to specific people to avoid politics. Just put them on a page in the report.

This kind of information is powerful since top leadership often don't get the chance to hear raw feedback that hasn't already been filtered through layers of management.

These concrete words often evoke an emotional reaction or connection and can be more influential than multiple pages of logical strategy.

The same can be said for using real world examples from your organization. Even a handful of good examples can make complex problems and solutions tangible, while also creating an emotional motivator for change.

Sometimes even the most thoroughly researched and detailed report fails to get traction because it doesn't generate an emotional connection that stimulates the will to change. Do both. Get the facts and position the findings in a way that compels the organization to change for good. That's good marketing after all, isn't it?

After you've finished gathering data, you'll need to analyze it and draw some conclusions on what you've seen and heard. The conclusions that you draw should then be prioritized in terms of business impact.

We recommend putting these findings into a document that also describes the approach you've used, who you spoke to, what you found, and some initial recommendations. This document will usually then feed into a formal check-in with leadership and be shared with some of the people you met with in the Data stage. This is particularly the case if your review is high priority/visibility due to business issues or will form the basis of a later investment in technology.

Even if a formal check-in isn't required, we still recommend document-ing your findings moving forward.

The reason for this documentation is that it can be easy to forget details of what you've covered, and you don't want to have to go back and ask someone to repeat themselves. Often just sending your report (or parts of it) to key people you've spoken to can be a powerful signal that pro-gress is being made, and things are changing.

Secondly, there might be a time gap between completing the Data stage and moving on to Design. This is often the case when the analysis shows the need for a system solution, and a system selection process is run. You'll want to be able to refer to your notes, and also use those notes to remind others of what was discussed, and what was found or agreed on.

In the process of prioritizing findings, we often try to identify "quick wins." These quick wins are usually small, cheap, and fast; and usually manifest in decisions or changes that can immediately improve the cur-rent situation.

The quick wins technique avoids the overreliance on expensive techno-logical solutions that will take months or years to implement, thus losing any momentum the initiative has accumulated. For example, a quick win might be to add a person to the distribution list for a report or email list. It could also be to allow a Marketing person to attend a regular Sales meeting, or something similar.

Quick wins are often simply a natural byproduct of being able to study an area in detail and having a forum to decide and fix these things that doesn't usually exist within the normal day to day of business operations, particularly at companies early on their journey. Later, as the company begins to adopt a change and continuous improvement culture, it will become the norm that personnel will be looking for and suggesting improvement opportunities, then fixing them, without having to formally launch a project to do so.

Concrete actions

While the Data stage will be slightly different depending on the scale of opportunity you're pursuing, the essence of this stage involves executing the data gathering/meetings plan we've been talking about in this chapter.

In addition, you can also take the following concrete actions:

- Develop a one-page overview of current processes: Customer Acquisition, Customer Retention, and Customer Expansion along with gaps in process and opportunities.
- Summarize and document your findings and recommendations.
- Test your findings with leadership and gauge level of interest and priority. Is there something that can and should be turned into a formal project?
- Identify quick wins and implement them.

Case Study - Applying the Theory

In the case study, the Align stage has been completed successfully. Key stakeholders are supportive of moving to the next stage, Data.

For your organization, write 5-10 bullet points that represent the key areas of work for the Data stage. Also quickly list out the types of information you will need to gather, from whom, and identify any difficulties you might anticipate in executing the plan.

Case Study - Data Stage Outcomes

Based on the conversations and completion of the "10 component" audit, the assessment was that Marketing was currently at "Crawl" level of maturity with some aspects of "Walk" overall.

Although the organization is a sizable and mature business, the Marketing team was positioned as a service function supporting sales and product teams by running events, creating brochures, email campaigns, and pushing out product related press releases. Marketing KPIs and success was measured based on the number of activities in the market, leads generated, and budget spent. The Marketing team began the year with a defined plan but it was Sales dictating which events, what brochures, etc. There was no alignment around buyer and customer personas. The Marketing organization sent out almost one million emails in twelve months. The Sales team was focused on selling features and benefits, not solutions. The result - siloed and disconnected teams with friction and frustration. Marketing was viewed as a cost-center and the first to experience cuts.

The audit identified the following key overarching issues:

- The organization was product centric.
- There was overreliance on existing customers and core markets, leaving them in reactive mode when growth slowed.
- There was poor alignment with Sales and the relationship was transactional.

- The organization experienced an overwhelming lack of customer centricity and market insights.
- Immature data strategy and governance made analytics and reporting challenging.

Since the Marketing team lacked strategic direction and structure, they only executed some basic process mapping around key marketing areas. This included: buyer personas, buyer journey mapping, demand generation foundations, integrated campaign framework and processes, lead management, and events.

Case Study - Discussion

The power of using a framework such as RVC shouldn't be underestimated. In the case study, it allowed the findings to be presented with a strong sense of objectivity and structure, rather than coming across as a personal agenda, or attack on other functions. The "one million emails" is a startling number not in a good way, particularly given that organizations may only have tens or hundreds of key/target accounts.

Those types of headline numbers and examples are not atypical for an organization at lower levels of maturity and can provide punchy reminders of the need to focus, and to change. You can only get those headline examples by speaking to people and looking at the data. While your data analysis must be sufficient to satisfy the organization that the data can be trusted, at least directionally, it doesn't pay to try to "boil the ocean" or get caught up in "analysis paralysis." Better to supplement a basic analysis with key headline numbers and stories that pack an emotional punch and crystallize the need to change in the minds of key stakeholders. Everyone hates email spam, and the organization was spamming its customers badly. This suggestion does not take away from the fact that you'll likely be performing a business case exercise later anyway that will detail the cost and size of both the problem and solution.

Chapter Conclusion

There is a natural and constant tendency to believe that the organization can build the future without understanding the present and this can result in initiatives failing due to lack of the right context and scope.

Instead of shooting from the hip, we suggest using the Data stage to build a fact base and gain alignment around the true underlying issues and the value of solving these.

Change is coming at such a rapid rate that we can find ourselves building mud on top of mud. There is no foundation. This is why it is so important to maintain a discipline around process mapping and documenting your analysis and findings. These create momentum, and feed into producing a quality blueprint for the future.

13

Design

Design is the process of creating a tangible *blueprint* for how Marketing and the organization will work to achieve overall growth objectives. The future vision for "why" the organization exists, and "what" the organization needs to do at the strategic level, will be converted into the detailed "how" and "who."

By the time you get to the Design stage, you will already have some idea of what the ultimate solution (e.g., process, structure, and technology changes) might be based on past experience, the vision that was outlined in the Align stage, and building on what you found in the Data stage. You won't be starting from a blank page.

For example, perhaps the organizational vision is to implement GX to drive sustainable growth. During the Data stage the existing revenue generating processes were mapped, and the gaps identified. Design is about generating options for closing the gap (the "O" in GROW) and detailing the approach that best satisfies various requirements.

The approach so far has involved a cross section of personnel in identifying the fundamental issues and opportunities.

Now, it's time to involve them in designing the solution.

Continuing involvement and collaboration with other functions is important, as the ideal solution for Marketing might be different from Sales' or IT's ideal solution, which might be different from what is best for the organization overall. The Design process seeks to explore and align these different perspectives into a single agreed upon solution or strategy that tries to optimize the overall benefits for the organization.

What Design looks like varies based on the nature of the strategy you are trying to implement and whether a technological solution is involved.

Most often, there will be a design resource or team who will organize design workshops to understand how the future business will operate. This includes how revenue generating processes will work, what the future roles and responsibilities will be, and where work will take place. This role is a specialized skill so might be played by an external consultant or facilitator if the skills don't exist in house.

In the case of using AGM to develop a new marketing strategy, you will use the Design stage to detail out what that strategy and associated plans will look like.

In the case of a transformation project, you will need to clearly articulate what is changing as well as document future processes and structures.

This answers both what is and isn't changing. Terms such as "transformation" can bring resistance due to the perception that everything will change, which may cause a lot of potential disruption.

Really, transformation is about getting a step-change in results. That step-change in results often originates from a very focused intervention on a specific business element. Explaining that 90% of current processes won't change can help put stakeholder's minds at ease. Outlining what is not changing also gives space to acknowledge what is working well today, and that the efforts in the past to develop those effective processes won't be "thrown away."

A common way of representing this "From:To" is to create a two-column table labeled by process or activity area. On the left will be "From," which represents the current way of working. On the right the "To" represents how that will work in the future.

Typical Activities

The typical activities in Design include:

- Identifying and documenting detailed requirements of how the future solution will work to meet vision, goals, and objectives.
- Identifying different solution options that trade off cost, complexity, fit with objectives
- Selecting the solution that best meets a prioritization of these criteria.
- Resolving design issues around how things will work, and work together across functions and teams.
- Creating a future strategy or blueprint referencing the ten RVC dimensions.

- Piloting, getting feedback, and iterating solutions before final approval.

In Practice

Design involves getting a clear perspective of the new requirements and capabilities needed to support organizational objectives and growth. By getting a clear picture of the future, you will then work backwards to what needs to change from today to enable that future.

The "problem" in design is different from simply the aggregate of issues you found in the Data stage. It is a valuable opportunity to explore possibility and opportunity and make not only a step but a step-change in organizational performance and outcomes. It is not about producing glossier product brochures but changing up the customer conversation completely. You'll want to design a solution that not only solves the problems of yesterday but accounts for the needs of the next 3-5 years.

It is also key not to be constrained by the old way of doing things, particularly if your organization's current situation matches many of the "descending" practices you read about in Part One.

Remember that these future requirements go into documenting the "target" for the design process. At the start of design, you probably won't know exactly how to implement these requirements. That is exactly the purpose of design, to get the "unconstrained" perspective on what the organization needs to be successful in terms of capabilities, and *then* explore different approaches for meeting those requirements, which trade off factors such as speed, cost, and functionality/fit.

The reason we're spending time outlining the thought process behind Design is that we often see organizations take shortcuts in the solutions process and come up with a "future" that is not only unexciting, but also doesn't deliver the benefits of sustainable growth. For example, you might find a way to better target end users of your solution (incremental change) but miss the opportunity to target the "C" level within your customers and build larger and more strategic relationships.

You might be solving a lot of problems, but not the ones that generate real value for the organization. You might even find yourself designing a solution that is already out of date by the time it is implemented.

There are different approaches to design consisting of various numbers of steps and stages. For example, the stages in Design Thinking include: Empathize, Define, Ideate, Prototype, and Test. Other approaches explicitly include stages such as Research, Selecting the Solution, and Learning. If you're implementing a systems solution, that might come with its own, or a third-party design approach.

To focus our discussion about Design, we'll concentrate on three areas:

1. Define – devising a clear statement of the problem and key requirements to fix it
2. Ideate – identifying different solutions and approaches to tackling the problem
3. Test – real world testing, feedback, and refinement of the solution

Let's discuss each now.

1. Define

A good design, as we've said, should not only fix yesterday's and today's problems, but also move the business forward towards growth. To do this at the start of the Design stage, you'll need to step away from the Data stage and regain sight of the big picture.

You may be inclined to say at the start of Design "we found an issue over there, let's direct our design effort at solving that issue." That is logical, but not always the best approach. Instead, it is often better to say "yes, we've found a problem over there, but what are we *really* trying to achieve in this area?" "What is the potential we could achieve?" The historical problem is only one input into the future solution you'll design. Often, by focusing more broadly on objectives and capabilities you'll find a more elegant solution having additional benefits than simply solving each singular problem in isolation.

There is a famous story that illustrates the importance of finding the right problem, which is called the elevator problem. One variation goes as follows: residents were complaining of wait times for elevators in their apartment block. Management enlisted engineers to look for ways to speed up the elevators but no solutions were found. A meeting was held to tell staff to expect ongoing complaints. A staff member at the meeting had observed that the elevators were not always that slow, but instead people got bored waiting. The focus of problem solving moved from the elevators to the residents themselves. After brainstorming how to stop people getting bored, mirrors were installed in the lift lobbies and complaints "plummeted."

What we're talking about here is *reframing* the original problem in a way that enables a simpler or more valuable solution to be found. The ability to reframe effectively is a learned and valuable skill but even without being an expert in reframing it is valuable to be aware of the concept and know that there are usually many different possible solutions to any problem, and often the first solution identified is not always the best solution.

It is also important to remember that your Design will necessarily touch on one or more components of the RVC such as processes, structure, skills so you'll need to think through those aspects in understanding issues and opportunities and building a complete solution.

Part of the "reset" between Data stage and Design is to be strategic and take a "top-down" approach to which *capabilities* need to be put in place to meet the future business requirements for growth. At this stage, it makes sense to identify a set of design principles to guide the solution, and the "From:To" format can be used to help devise these principles.

For example, perhaps the Data stage found misalignment due to different parts of the business seeing different versions of customer data. This misalignment represents the current situation or "From." situation. Instead of diving in to fix all the data issues with "Report X", you might first identify an overarching design principle such as having a "single source of truth" for customer data, priority accounts, personas. A design principle cuts across different areas of the future design and provides guidance and a lens to look at the final solution. For example, a great design is not just about fixing "Report X", it is about looking at the processes and people that surround the report and how they must adapt to support "one version of the truth".

Alignment itself might be a design principle. For example, once the design team works out the new required capabilities, the principle of alignment, and alignment steps/touchpoints should be built into the supporting processes for those new capabilities.

Here some examples of requirements for growth and related potential solutions:

- Ability to talk about a prospect's business and how our solution will help generate business value. Potential solution: moving from product to solution selling.
- Ability to identify new markets and customers to support growth. Potential solutions: targeting, account-based marketing, and customer diversification process.
- Growing revenue from existing customers. Potential solutions: customer retention, customer expansion, and building customer lifetime value.

You decide at a summary level what needs to be done in the future, think about options of how to achieve that, and finally work out the detailed "what" and "who" of the chosen solution.

Solution selling, for example, involves putting in place the right approach, process, skills, resources, planning and capabilities. A capability is simply the mix of things that have to be in place to be able to sustainably do an important thing and do it well each time.

Often, you'll start the Design stage by coming up with a list of principles for how the future solution will work.

For example, you might have a principle relating to only having one list of focus accounts across Sales and Marketing. Alignment and Integration might be another design principle. These represent the rules for how the future solution should work, so that you can use them to make decisions about its design.

Using the above example, how should you deal with the global team wanting to pitch focus accounts that don't match with the "one" list agreed on by Sales and Marketing? Because a principle has been written down a debate can be had about how to deal with global, rather than sleepwalking into approving exceptions that water down the solution.

In the case of designing for a transformation project, it is essential to discuss and get agreement early in the design stage for the list of the key capabilities required to support future growth. There are many capabilities that the organization *could* invest in, so it is important to focus and be clear that the list of capabilities agreed on represents the best business value.

Often the design team or Marketing will create a summary picture of these new capabilities. This can be done at a high-level capability or process area or by adding bullet points to the RVC to show the new capabilities that are required in each of the 10 areas.

Implicit in the design and deployment of any capability, is how best to deliver it given several options. Should this capability be outsourced, partially filled with third party resources, or placed in a regional or global center? The capabilities are identified and designed in the "Define" step, and delivery options are explored in the "Ideate" step, which comes next.

2. Ideate

Ideate is the process of generating potential solutions, ideas, and designs that address the overarching problem and build required capabilities that you defined in the last step.

This ideation process will take place in one or several working sessions, attended by Sales, Marketing, Finance, and other parts of the business. Ideation is more than brainstorming; it is a facilitated process that incorporates various skill sets, domain knowledge, and ideation techniques. Ideation is about exploring options, challenging assumptions, constraints, and determining how things could and should best work in future.

It's common to give participants a pre-read or pre-briefing at least a few days before any working sessions. This pre-read will reiterate the business objectives, list of capabilities, key findings from the Data stage and any other relevant information including potential solutions and customer feedback.

If the capabilities that you are designing are customer facing, then you'll almost certainly want to get customer input at various stages in the Design process.

The basic unit of focus in design will be the revenue generating process. Once the activities required to generate growth have been discussed and documented, then the team can move on to other design elements such as roles and responsibilities, structure, and measures as part of 10 areas within the RVC.

One thing to be avoided in the Design stage is building a "field of dreams." Left unchecked, various stakeholders will inevitably try to get their entire "wishlist" into the final design.

The design team will need to be rigorous in prioritizing candidate requirements in terms of business impact, solution complexity, etc. Specifically, there is a direct connection between requirements and Service Level Agreements.

It might be tempting to say that Marketing will agree to everything, but this is impractical. You need to make it clear that prioritized requirements will be scrutinized for feasibility.

It is also important to set expectations that new requirements will be phased in during different stages of Deployment. The whole solution likely won't be available on day one, but the core requirements will be delivered first, and then the solution will be built out in phases from there.

Having these scope and priority "debates" early and often helps increase the likelihood of success of the initiative, since expectations are managed sooner and there are "no surprises" at the Deployment stage. Better to be crystal clear on what is and isn't in the solution, and deal with issues early on.

3. Test

Modern design practices almost always include a degree of prototyping, A/B testing or other real-world piloting before the design is locked. As experienced marketers, you'll have likely used these techniques around demand generation activities. The same type of flexibility and learning-by-doing is required when testing potential solutions and future ways of working.

While prototyping, you must ask yourself "is this sustainable?" Does the whole thing hang together? Have each of the 10 dimensions of the RVC been considered in coming up with the final design and/or strategy?

Often the "quick wins" we talked about, and a pilot program can go hand in hand.

Perhaps you've developed a temporary process for Sales and Marketing to work together on Account Based Marketing, while you develop the formal processes, systems, and role changes. This initial pilot can provide quick learnings, a much better understanding of the real requirements vs. desires, build confidence and momentum for the final solution.

A pilot can affect only a portion of customers and staff, with both Sales and Marketing agreeing to which customers and staff are involved. If necessary, staff involved in the pilot might need some relief from day-to-day tasks to allow the trial to not be sabotaged by "real work."

Concrete actions

The following concrete actions can be taken as part of the Design:

- Define the problem – frame the design problem in terms of the bigger picture (business objectives and vision) and what is required to support growth.
- Seek input – from customers and other parts of the business on potential solutions to the defined problem.

- Test – your ideas for potential solutions using a limited prototype or pilot, gain feedback and improve the solution.

Case Study - Applying the Theory

Reflect on a past change in your organization. Did it use a formal methodology to design the future processes and other aspects of the change? How did the approach differ from what you read in this chapter?

Case Study - Design Stage Outcomes

The priority was to revisit the foundations and re-energize the Marketing team. Next, the key internal Marketing processes were reviewed together with team roles and responsibilities. After that, the "external" touch points were defined in a workshop with Sales, including alignment on targets and KPIs, lead definition, buyer personas, sales and marketing plays, processes, reporting, and Service Level Agreements.

The Marketing leader went on a roadshow, both in person and virtual, met the different teams, evangelized the Marketing story, what was changing, why, and what it meant for them.

The business case for change was compelling because it contained data points around key Sales and Marketing challenges, such as opportunities missed, data issues, etc. This information was then used to create a full business case document that outlined the objectives, methodology, review, and scope for change, then proposed programs with investment and a three-year timeline.

The team developed a blueprint for change that closed the gaps between current vs. desired processes and existing capability gaps, then identified the building blocks of where Marketing and the organization needed to be. Key priorities were then set out as part of a three-year roadmap to change.

Phase One of the design would be to look at forming the basic building blocks of a revenue engine that could be scaled up later. This involved planning to build some integrated campaigns to test and learn while optimizing structure, putting in place the right processes, optimizing MAP/CRM, data, etc.

When it came to Customer Centric Marketing, as an example, there was a need to explain that future success for the organization starts with knowing the buyer in terms of the problems they face, their opportunities, goals, and the environment they operate in. This would be achieved through data, insights, journey mapping, personas, alignment, as well as upskilling the team.

Case Study - Discussion

An observation from the case is that it is important to not forget to focus on getting the Marketing team itself energized and ready for the change. You might think that Marketing will naturally be excited about stepping up, but with any change comes potential anxiety from the team.

A second note is that Service Level Agreements must be created or updated as the result of the new design. It is not enough to sit in a conference room and agree the new processes together, since the reality is that an evolution of the Marketing function will almost involve a refocusing and changes in existing ways of working. Some existing priority areas might be deprioritized or stopped altogether, and other new ones added and these need to be documented in black and white.

Chapter Conclusion

The design process is about identifying the capabilities required to support growth, and then configuring these in a way that the solution hangs together and is sustainable.

The design process, just like the growth engine, aims to ensure that multiple perspectives and considerations are incorporated into producing an implementable design that delivers growth.

The outputs from Part One of this book and prior experiences should be brought into the design process. A view of potential solutions should be developed that overcome some of the perceived limitations and constraints of the current situation and, importantly, build a solution for the next 3-5 years.

Lastly, designing the future can be exciting but keep an eye on implementation since it is better to have a working solution that you can deploy, than a field of dreams that can't be built.

14

Deploy

"A plan without action is not a plan. It's a speech."

Boone Pickens, Business magnate

The Deploy stage is about transitioning your ideas, strategies, and designs into action within the business.

What deploy looks and feels like, will differ depending on whether you are deploying a new marketing strategy, or selecting, configuring, and going-live with a new systems solution.

What remains the same for all deploy situations is the need for good project and change management, communications, and so on. You'll need to set up criteria that describe *what success looks like* at the end of deployment.

We already know that most projects fail to deliver the intended benefits. Marketing projects are not immune from these statistics. In our experience, it is common that Marketing projects are executed *without* dedicated resources and are often driven by the adoption of a specific technological solution. Insufficient effort is given to considering the integrated set of capabilities required to support growth in a sustainable way.

To counter these challenges, we've aimed to set you up for success with the AGM approach, so that you've followed through with critical tasks in a systematic and structured way.

Being set up for success is key, since the deploy stage is complex enough given the need to manage multiple workstreams, including possible technology and system integration projects.

Typical Activities

Deployment is about putting the design blueprint into practice.

If you are deploying a new strategy then your deployment will typically involve reworking the team and roles, utilizing new ways of working around Customer Knowledge, implementing changes to core revenue generating processes, and running the new Demand Generation activities for new customer and market groups.

Now let's look in more detail at Project Management, Change Management, and Communications aspects of Deploy.

Project Management

Even if your project doesn't merit a formal project manager, it is still necessary to manage all the moving parts it contains.

Teams need clarity around what is expected of them and when, particularly if they are juggling several other projects at the same time. You or a team member will need to play the role of project manager. In some cases, it might make sense to use a resource from the Sales team to manage the implementation of the project, particularly if you anticipate pushback from that team around new ways of working.

At a minimum, your deployment plan should include major milestones related to when various changes will go live. Cloud based tools such as Asana, Monday, Trello, and even Microsoft Excel are easy to use and can be suitable for this purpose if the organization doesn't have an existing project management tool. Your plan should also define the success criteria for each stage of deployment.

For example, new joint processes that Sales and Marketing will work on together will need to be scheduled to ensure people are available to do the work. The teams must have the expectation that not everything will go perfectly straight away, and that there is a need to work together to get the new solution up and running. A culture of constructive feedback where necessary should be cultivated.

Leaders must be on the lookout to ensure the team is adopting the new ways of working and intervene on issues as they arise.

The project plan will help drive both change management and communications as well, since these activities will be done in parallel with other project activities, rather than as an afterthought.

Change Management

As we mentioned above, change management is not something that is tacked on to a project, rather something embedded in how the project is run right from the start.

While project management is geared toward ensuring that a set of outputs are delivered on time and budget, change management involves ensuring that new strategies are implemented and new processes, systems, and reports are actually *used*.

The foundation of change management involves understanding *what* is changing and *when* and then to manage the impact of that on various stakeholders both inside and outside the business.

As we mentioned in the Align stage, we recommend that you create a stakeholder management plan early on and continue to work on it throughout the stages of AGM.

Have you moved all the "red" stakeholders to at least yellow if not green active supporters? The truth is that perhaps not everyone will become a huge advocate of what you are doing.

In many cases, it is enough if some stakeholders are "neutral" or simply don't act as a blocker. Having visible project and change management in place often goes a long way to help nervous stakeholders feel more comfortable with the change ahead.

In order to drive change, you need to find "change champions" in other teams that share your vision and can help advocate for your cause and support behavior shifts. For example, if you are piloting an ABM program, you may want to find Sales champions that are willing to be part of the pilot and share the success more broadly. In the case of a bigger transformation, you will need champions in different functions to drive this change.

Another foundation of change management is in the assessment of change readiness. Based on your understanding of what is changing, you try to identify potential issues with the organization's ability to successfully take on the new changes in process, systems, and so on.

Whenever you ask someone to do things differently there is always the possibility that they may be unable or unwilling to do so! You'll no doubt already have a detailed sense of your own team's capability in the Data stage and get a sense of willingness as the project proceeds through Design.

Because of this change management also often includes specific training and onboarding activities for staff. In parallel, you might have decided to shuffle roles with some staff departing and new faces arriving. The time to think about all of this is way before going live with the new processes!

Communications

Ironically, communication is often one of the most neglected areas of effecting change in Marketing. We can get caught up in the immense pressures of keeping Marketing's business-as-usual work ticking over while also trying to design and implement the future. These pressures might mean that we don't get around to communicating with the rest of the organization about the change, which is a key factor in making that change successful.

You might follow the maxim "communicate early and often!" While this is often true, an effective communications strategy has to be about *what the audience needs* rather than simply repeating yourself several times.

Because of this your communications strategy will be divided by stakeholder category and type of update.

While a memo might be effective for some communications, others might require a formal briefing or one-on-one meeting. In between these extremes are the familiar multimedia models of dissemination: videos, webinars, podcasts, etc.

Communications are always a combination of tell, sell, and ask as well. From a Sales perspective, it is important to remind people why change is necessary when the initial effort to transition gets overwhelming.

Take the time to identify some compelling key messages for what you are trying to do, and link that with the overarching changes in the market, evolving strategy and what's in it for the receiver of the communication. Remember, you will continue to market yourself, your team, and the solution through the deployment stage and into sustaining the benefits.

Although you'll have numerous checklists, deployment is never a checkbox exercise. Deployment can only be considered a success when new processes and systems are *used*, and the *benefits* begin to be delivered.

Therefore, it's important to revisit the success criteria established for the initiative, both from the perspective of process metrics as well as outcomes. You should anticipate the need to monitor and even "babysit" the new process to iron out any teething troubles, taking corrective action as required.

Case Study - Applying the Theory

Describe your view of the key activities required for successful deployment in 5-10 bullet points. Thinking back to a previous project deployment at your organization, what went right and what went wrong? What would you do differently next time, based on the information in this chapter?

Case Study - Deploy Stage Outcomes

Moving from Design to Deploy was like the continuation of an ongoing conversation. One that had started before the role was even hired. The principles for what the future would look like had stayed the same the whole time. The difference was that now the organization was coming along on the journey. Various teams had input in the future design of the principles in detail and in *practice* at *this* organization.

Leadership held sessions during Deploy to build Sales and Marketing alignment, the actual personas, and Ideal Customer Profiles, and begin to establish Service Level Agreements, etc.

As a result of the successful alignment during the Design process, a separate business case was identified, and approved, for introducing the sales development function to support outbound prospecting, lead qualification and pipeline acceleration.

In addition, training on the new concepts and processes was rolled out to the broader team, and a marketing playbook was developed that outlined their goals. During this time, it was still necessary to frame what was changing in terms of "leading practices." For example, referring to various third-party sources to give the broader team some comfort that this new direction wasn't "bleeding edge" but, by that time, common industry practice.

Part of the stakeholder engagement strategy was called a "big rocks" approach, based on the analogy of putting sand, small rocks, and big rocks in a jar. That is, if you start filling the jar with the sand and the small rocks, then there will be no room to fit in the important "big rocks."

The Marketing team was changing from focusing on sand, to focusing on rocks. This message was both for internal and external consumption. Some other parts of the organization had been relying on Marketing to do their work, so this was a message that priorities were changing.

To support that change, a list of key priorities was created by Marketing in discussion with other functions and communicated to the broader organization to coincide with change of job descriptions and team structure in Marketing.

There were other communications that went out to the organization that built transparency over what Marketing was doing, why, and which leadership had been involved. These communications were also a heads-up that further projects were still in the pipeline. It also showed that this was an ongoing process of change that would bring positive benefits not just to Sales and Marketing, but to the whole organization.

Change to the Marketing organizational structure was critical. It was important to understand people in their current roles, their skills, talents, and aspirations. From there we answered questions such as "How can we deploy them in this new environment and what's needed to make them successful?"

The key to bringing the team on this journey was for them to become part of the vision. Unfortunately, even though they bought into the vision and were excited about the future, some of them resisted change and ultimately left.

In hindsight the initial assessment back in the Data and Align stages had already flagged team issues which should have been acted on then. However, there was the thought of giving the team the chance to step up. There was also a desire to not rock the boat too much too early on as well as a fear of acting quickly on what was already clear in hindsight.

This decision cost six months of lost progress until the right team could be hired. The whole transformation could have been faster and more successful if the right people had been on board early.

In the case study, the organization moved from one MAS to another since the former was too complex and no one knew how to operate it.

Secondly, the team only used the old system for sending emails and not integrated campaigns, so it was a waste of resources. The key is to understand how the system feeds and supports the full customer lifecycle and then map and build it into your strategy.

The other common issue is that marketing teams lack a proper Martech strategy or technologists, so technology is usually owned by marketing operations or demand teams who lack the expertise to build effective technology stacks. MAS should be part of a broader digital transformation strategy.

The Critical Success Factors for getting deployment right were:

- Strategy - Building the deployment plan on a deep understanding of the current situation. Having a full 360 view, understanding the relevant maturity level of the organization, means you can set the right level of ambition and assistance, then articulate the right strategy and change management programs.

- People - Having the right people in place; once the right talent was on board, it was easy to accelerate and scale.

- Culture - Team had to share the same vision and be in it for the long haul. It was about teamwork and winning together. Also having a growth mindset! It's easy to get stuck in the old way of doing things. When challenged, people need to step up.

- Communication - Not just communicating with the Marketing team but the broader organization as well. This role became the "evangelist" for what the transformation was trying to do to support the organization. This meant constantly communicating, sharing wins, and securing buy-in at the leadership level. This also meant celebrating small wins and sharing successes and team functions with the broader organization.

- Transparency. Being open about the challenges, whether it's the Marketing team's own shortcomings, data issues, process gaps, or issues with Sales such as leads not progressing. All of this was backed up with facts and not opinion. It was always critical to back claims with data or other people's validation.

The first thing that went "wrong" was getting the right team in place. As mentioned before, the approach was to give the team the benefit of the doubt and not be so aggressive in pushing the agenda. This situation was remedied by hiring a new team.

Some of the initial campaigns didn't deliver the expected ROI so this was addressed by developing plays and constant optimization. Having an agile approach and constantly improving became a key mantra.

How did you measure success in deployment?

Success was measured by reporting on the key metrics and KPIs as set out in the plan. The first point was the success of campaigns in terms of contribution. Key rev gen metrics also began to be reported such as opportunity generation, win rates, and new logos.

Some of the successes:

- Delivered a 30% increase in revenue on the previous year within 12 months, attributable to marketing activity.
- Generated a multimillion-dollar pipeline of qualified opportunities within a one-year period by building a sales development team from the ground up and connecting marketing strategy and campaigns with sales strategy.
- Facilitated 200% growth in the region qualified leads by transforming Go-To-Market strategy for one the key solutions, by leveraging sales enablement on a global level.
- Achieved 80% customer retention rate.

Case Study - Discussion

The Deploy stage requires discipline and accountability. This is where we put all the plans into action. If transformation happens at the departmental level, the head of the department naturally becomes the lead that drives all the changes needed. If the transformation happens at the organizational level, it is critical to appoint a change leader and this person should possess leadership skills and be empowered from top-down to own actions. Like managing any project there should be a project plan with clear actions and milestones, as well as how we measure success. The measurement is critical as this helps with the next phase: Sustain.

The Deploy stage can take anywhere from six months to a couple of years depending on the scope of change and speed by which things happen. It's important to share the small wins early and build confidence in the program. What ultimately drives success is leadership and stakeholder management so deploying the age-old "managing up, down, and sideways" needs to be a perfected art.

It's important to have found and re-energized any ambassadors or champions before getting into deployment. You can't be everywhere, and you'll rely on these supporters to engage with the solutions and fix problems, or at least make sure problems are brought to your attention rather than being left to fester. You can also find a junior resource to take the role of analyst/facilitator to help identify and document "bugs," and hopefully to help the new solution stick.

Chapter Conclusion

The real measure of success in the Deploy stage is not only that new ideas and projects have gone live but that Marketing and the organization are set up to reap the benefits.

While the approach and methodology to deployment will differ depending on the scope and nature of the project or strategy, what will remain the same is the need to address Project Management, Change Management, and Communications.

Deployment is not the end of the work! The solution must not only be deployed but also successfully transitioned into business as usual. That is the role of the Sustain stage.

15

Sustain

"Life begins at the end of your comfort zone."

Neale Donald Walsch, Author

The Sustain stage is about maintaining momentum towards realizing the full potential of, and benefits from, the strategy or solution, and managing the transition of the solution from initiative to business as usual.

There is a tendency to feel that once a new strategy, process or system is deployed, and the champagne corks have been popped, that all the hard work is done.

In reality, all we have achieved at that point is the organizational equivalent of going to the gym every day for the first two weeks of January. It is an achievement, sure, but not yet enough to change your life.

Ultimate success will come from making the new level of effort your default and fixing any "bugs" that jeopardize results as well as setting a plan for continual improvement.

Despite the importance of what we've just discussed, the Sustain stage is often neglected or skipped entirely, and as a result the success of the project is left to chance rather than intent.

Typical Activities

In this chapter we'll talk about three key aspects of Sustain:

1. Transitioning the strategy or solution to Business as Usual (BAU)
2. Managing performance and benefits realization
3. Continuous improvement

In Practice

The underlying philosophy of Sustain is that offense is the best form of defense. Rather than wait for problems to pop up, be proactive. Let's look at each of the three aspects now.

1. Transitioning the strategy/solution to Business as Usual (BAU)

We've all been there. The regular meetings that had been part of developing and rolling out the strategy stop. The project team, if you had one, has rolled off or gone back to focus on their day jobs. And organizational priorities move on to the next thing.

We've heard this feeling at the end of a project likened to a leadership "lighthouse beacon." For a while you are in the focal point of the bright light, all expectations, attention, and support are on you.

Then the beam swings around to something else, the next "shiny" area, or crisis requiring leadership attention. Suddenly, your calls don't get responded to as quickly, or at all.

Without focus and a proactive approach, the inevitable challenges that pop up risk sabotaging the new strategy even as it shows initial promise. This can cause the organization to slip back to its old ways.

These challenges include things like:

- Teething troubles related to the new process of doing things
- Systems and data issues
- Manual work and workarounds causing fatigue or errors
- Old and new processes continuing to run parallel causing confusion and duplicated effort
- A crisis causes a return to old habits and ways of working
- The pilot fizzles out and never scales up

In fact, these challenges occur so frequently that you should anticipate them, define them as risks to the project, and manage them proactively. Good practice suggests a 4-6 week post implementation support period, followed by a formal post implementation or action review.

During the support period, the team will be actively soliciting feedback from stakeholders in the new strategy/solution, be on the lookout for issues, and be in problem solving mode.

In addition to generalized support, we'd like to call out three specific areas to look at:

i. Evaluating the pilot

ii.   Phasing out manual, temporary, or old processes

iii. Managing moments of truth

i. Pilot

In the case of a limited pilot, you will need to set a date and agree on success criteria and what should happen next.

In the Sustain stage, you'll review the pilot and agree either to scale it up, tweak or continue it, or go back to the drawing board entirely.

Scaling up the rollout of a strategy will likely involve a return to earlier stages like further design tweaking and will certainly require the same disciplines found in deployment.

ii. Phasing out manual, temporary, or old processes

The Sustain stage is the time to do housekeeping of all types.

In the Deploy phase you might have planned manual processes that allowed the strategy or solution to go live on time. In addition to that, other unplanned manual processes might be added as workarounds to bugs found in deployment. These workarounds also need to move to a permanent solution.

For example, you might have decided to continue both old and new planning processes in parallel to mitigate the risk of the new process failing. In Sustain you must remember to go back and formally review and approve the new process to decommission the old one. If you ask a team to generate new reports in addition to the old ones, then you need to remember to go back and eliminate the old reports if the new ones are satisfactory.

You might find that old ways of working persist after the cutover. For example, people may still be using old templates, processes, or reverting to old roles, etc. You will need to be on the lookout for this and get to the bottom of the issues such as training, habits, or conflicting goals and fix these.

As mentioned in the Deploy stage, we often rely on change champions in the organization to help us smooth the path to new ways of working. Change champions are the people on the team that are tasked with leading by example. They are critical in phasing out old behaviors and can act as monitors or guides to other people on the team. Change champions however are not a substitute for employee training and/or effective system design and implementation.

iii. Managing moments of truth

A true measure of any or behavioral change is what happens in times of crisis.

Do people stick with the new way or revert to old habits? The tendency is for humans to return to old habits even if intellectually we know that these are not what we are supposed to be doing.

You might also have to politely remind leadership what they'd agreed to in supporting the new process, and that backtracking in times of crisis will not only sabotage this project but jeopardize trust and the ability to make changes in future.

2. Managing performance and benefits realization

Managing performance and benefits realization is about taking a high-level look at the new strategy or solution in terms of desired vs. actual outcomes and benefits.

Perhaps people are using the new process, but you are not yet getting the anticipated traction on benefits.

Sometimes this lack of traction is due to the natural learning curve of anything new. Over time both efficiency and effectiveness will increase. Many tech companies have customer success roles aiming to improve adoption rate. We understand that if customers are not using our solution, they are not going to renew. With core systems it is the same, our job is only done when we remove the barriers to operating in the new way.

At other times benefits will be dependent on several factors happening and perhaps one or more of these factors hasn't yet taken place.

Continuing the gym example from earlier: perhaps you started at the gym to lose weight, but although you're working out, you haven't changed your diet or other parts of your lifestyle.

Sometimes, despite best intentions, understanding the complete set of factors that drive benefits is a learning process that happens over time. Perhaps new information on requirements comes to light that means part of the solution will be redesigned.

A common example is when a business case is based on decommissioning an old system, but after going live, that the system is still used for a critical but previously unknown process. It can't be decommissioned, and the benefits can't be realized, until a new solution meets the requirements that were satisfied by the old system. Or through the design process, those requirements can be challenged, changed, or eliminated.

The same applies to the work of teams. Perhaps "critical" tasks that are holdovers from the old structure are preventing the team from thinking and working strategically in the new structure.

Change is hard, so we need to leave some room for mistakes and allow for a buffer to fix them.

The key is to create an environment where we can talk honestly about successes and failures and take actions to improve accordingly. Without authenticity, we will not get there. Leaders can create a culture that promotes that authenticity, or they can create a finger-pointing environment that prevents honest dialogue within the company.

What happens if things don't go to plan? Is that failure or learning?

One of the most unexpected things to deal with as an Ascending Marketer is your own perfectionism! As a team member you probably set impossibly high standards for the quality of your outputs and put in the work to deliver on that.

As a manager, you no-doubt learned that not everyone has the same standards as you, and you can't be a taskmaster all the time. Transitioning to a more senior role can rekindle these perfectionist impulses. After all, your name is on the line! As you set expectations with yourself and others it is productive to also keep the right perspective on when things don't work as planned.

You could see setbacks as a failure, or you can see it as a learning opportunity. The reality is that you can't play it safe and still grow, whether we are talking about organizations, teams, or individuals.

3. Continuous improvement

Continuous improvement is about embedding a culture of measurement and improvement within Sales, Marketing, and the organization. We know that change is a constant, so while deploying a single strategy or project is important, what is transformational is the ability to triage and deliver change on an ongoing basis.

This is about getting the "building blocks" in place for cross-functional working and project and change management, as well as sustaining the relationships that go along with that.

You might be familiar with the cycle of Plan, Do, Review (PDR) as applied to continuous improvement. First you plan what you'll do, then you'll do the work, then you'll review what you just did and make the necessary adjustments feeding back into the next cycle of PDR.

PDR can be applied to a systems implementation, strategy, activity, or even a single conversation with the customer. It is good discipline for when Sales and Marketing begin to work together and will drive discipline in planning. The process of debriefing will quickly highlight differing expectations and perceptions that need to be discussed and aligned.

In addition to new ideas, it is likely there will be a host of good ideas that you weren't able to put into action in the initial strategy deployment. Before these inputs get lost it is important to ensure that they are cataloged, prioritized, and stored for when you return to "Phase 2."

Finally, an important element of continuous improvement is always having an eye on the future. This tranche of effort might have gotten the organization from crawl to walk, but other possibilities and opportunities remain to further increase maturity down the line.

"The only thing that doesn't change is change itself" - Louis L'Amour

Change never stops! With the pace of technology, transformation and disruption happening across industries, marketers are at the forefront of change. Whether it's a change of business model, need for diversification or adoption of new technology, Marketing leaders are always leading and managing progress.

Most successful leaders we've seen are also great learners, adopting a habit of lifelong curiosity.

Whether you manage change well or not you are creating a legacy for whomever comes next.

So, the question is what kind of legacy do you want to leave behind?

Case Study - Applying the Theory

Think about a previous change at your organization where the benefits were not sustained. What happened? What would the organization need to do differently based on what you've read in this chapter?

Case Study - Outcomes from Sustain stage

The idea of lifelong learning and continuous improvement was formally baked into the program.

For example, continuous improvement steps included:

- Adopting agile marketing ways of working
- Win/loss reviews on activity
- Performance reviews
- Lunch & learn sessions for Marketing
- Ongoing market insights and customer visits

Case Study - Discussion

The Marketing leader that led the successful transformation moved on some time after implementation and, although there was momentum from everything that had been put in place, a change of business leadership meant a change in direction. The consequences of not maintaining a continuous improvement standard are a workforce that becomes disengaged with decreased productivity and customers looking elsewhere for similar products or services from competitors who respond to their changing needs.

Conclusion

Continuing our gym example, *not* engaging with the Sustain stage is like going to the gym for a month then saying "I've done it. Fitness is now mine for life!"

In reality, benefits come from sustained effort over time, the building of new habits and the avoidance of pitfalls and distractions. It is important to build continuous improvement into the culture of your organization. After being through the whole AGM process at least once, your team and the organization should clearly see the benefits of working in new ways to get new results.

Organizations we've worked with see continuous improvement as a source of company pride, but pride that is *curious* first rather than arrogant. It becomes natural and expected to hear improvement suggestions coming from all parts and levels of the organization.

As we've said throughout the book, almost everything in business is a cycle. Your work won't stop at the Sustain stage. The environment, customers, and competitors will change. What was once leading practice will become the norm.

At that point you will, in effect, move back to the Align stage again.

You'll establish a new vision of the future and quantify the gap between that and where you are today, then help the organization to take the next leap forward.

16

Elevate One Million

"When the whole world is silent, even one voice becomes powerful."

Malala Yousafzai, Activist

In this book we've asked you to step up both at work and in life.

This is not just a book about Marketing. Neither is it the final word, rather the start of a conversation. Our mission is to enable a new generation of leaders who not only care about work, but the world, taking on the social, political, and environmental challenges of today and tomorrow, and changing the world of work for the better.

If we didn't believe that, and act on it, then you wouldn't be holding this book in your hands. What gets us out of bed in the morning is the feeling that we are using our abilities and experience to make a difference.

All paths are paved with trial and tribulation, surprise, and uncertainty. We invite you to join the Ascending Growth community and share your journey, experiences and learnings. **To find out more please visit** www.ascendinggrowh.com

You are the storytellers. So, change the story.

Be the hero of the growth story that you create.

* * *

Epilogue

Wings flutter away rising steam and spray from morning rain showered streets. Gotham yellow cabs fleeting. This city. This. Eyes now focus on flapping and floating forms gliding freely up among looming skyscrapers. Painted silver metal birds journeying yet higher, from there to here and everywhere.

Glossary

Term	Definition
Account Based Marketing (ABM)	A business-to-business (B2B) strategy that focuses sales and marketing resources on target accounts within a specific market.
Acquisition Strategy	A sales strategy that articulates the WHAT and HOW of a revenue target that can be delivered from acquiring new customers.
Agile Marketing	An approach to marketing that utilizes the principles and practices of agile methodologies. This includes having self-organizing, cross-functional teams doing work in frequent iterations with continuous feedback.
AI	Artificial Intelligence is the ability of a digital computer or computer-controlled robot to perform tasks commonly associated with intelligent beings.
Ascending Growth Method (AGM)	A 5-step circular change implementation methodology designed to help cross functional teams to effectively identify problems

	to solve, align team members towards common goals in order to make the necessary changes, and assist the team to develop the action plan to implement and improve continuously.
B2B	B2B stands for Business-to-business marketing. It refers to the marketing of products or services to other businesses and organizations.
B2C	B2C or business to consumer, is the type of commerce transaction in which businesses sell products or services directly to consumers.
Branding	Branding is the process with a series of activities a business performs to make itself known to the public and differentiates itself from competitors.
Cost to Serve	The measurement of cost factors that go into the servicing of a customer, or the production of a product.
Customer Lifetime Value (CLV)	A measure of the average customer's revenue generated over their entire relationship with a company.

Customer Relationship Management (CRM)	A technology for managing all your company's relationships and interactions with customers and potential customers.
Customer Satisfaction Score (CSAT)	Short for customer satisfaction score. It's a commonly used metric that acts as a key performance indicator for customer service and product quality in all kinds of businesses.
Demand Shaping	Demand shaping is the influencing of demand to match planned supply.
Enterprise Resource Planning (ERP)	A technology that organizations use to manage day-to-day business activities such as accounting, procurement, project management, risk management and compliance, and supply chain operations.
Expansion Strategy	A sales strategy that articulates the WHAT and HOW of a revenue target that can be delivered from expanding share of wallet from existing customers.
Go-To-Market (GTM) Strategy	GTM is a plan that details how an organization can engage with customers to convince them to buy their product or service and to gain a competitive advantage.
GROW	Created by Sir John Whitmore in the late 1980s, the GROW model is a coaching

	framework used in conversations and everyday leadership to unlock potential and possibilities. GROW stands for Goal, Reality, Options, and Will.
Growth Experience (GX)	A managerial framework that helps senior leadership to understand that sustainable growth can only be achieved at the intersection of organizational, customer, and people growth.
GXO	Growth Experience Officer
ICT	Information and Communication Technology
Ideal Customer Profile (ICP)	A description of the company — not the individual buyer or end user — that's a perfect fit for your solution.
Inverted pyramids	A leadership style that puts more focus on employees who directly add value to the customer's happiness with the company.
Key Performance Indicators (KPIs)	A quantifiable measure of performance over time for a specific objective.
Marketing Qualified Lead (MQL)	A potential customer that has been reviewed by the marketing team and satisfies

	the criteria necessary to be passed along to the sales team.
Martech	A set of software solutions used by Marketing leaders to support mission-critical business objectives and drive innovation within their organizations.
MAS (Marketing Automation Software)	Applications that help automate your marketing practices including email marketing, lead nurturing, scoring, and grading, social posting, and reporting.
Net Promoter Score (NPS)	NPS stands for Net Promoter Score which is a metric used in customer experience programs. NPS measures the loyalty of customers to a company.
Persona Profiles	A detailed, fictitious portrait of marketing targets: who they are, their tastes, habits, needs, pain points etc.
Personalization	The practice of using data to deliver brand messages targeted to an individual prospect.
PESTEL Analysis	A strategic framework commonly used to evaluate the business environment in which a firm operates. PESTEL is an acronym for Political, Economic, Social, Technological, Environmental and Legal factors. PESTEL was invented in 1967 by Francis Aguilar

	who was an American scholar whose expertise was in strategic planning.
Power distance	A term that describes how people belonging to a specific culture view power relationships - superior/subordinate relationships - between people, including the degree that people not in power accept that power is spread unequally.
RACI	A responsibility assignment matrix that details how various roles will participate in completing a projects' tasks or deliverables.
Retention Strategy	A sales strategy that articulates the WHAT and HOW of a revenue target that can be delivered from retaining existing customers.
Revenue Generation Value Chain (RVC)	A business management concept that was first developed by Eve Chen in 2015. RVC is a value chain that comprises a collection of activities under ten practice areas that are performed by a company to create customer value and improve the organization's ability to generate revenues.
S&OP	Sales and operations planning is an integrated business management process that drives organizational consensus to balance supply and demand.

Sales Accepted Lead (SAL)	An MQL that has been passed on to the sales team and met the agreed-upon criteria for sales-readiness.
Sales Qualified Lead (SQL)	A lead your sales team has qualified as a potential customer.
SDR	A sales development representative is an individual who focuses on prospecting, moving, and qualifying leads through the sales pipeline and then delivers those leads to individuals who are responsible for closing sales.
Segmentation	A marketing strategy that creates subsets of a market based on demographics, needs, priorities, common interests and other psychographic or behavioral criteria used to better understand the target audience.
SEO	Search Engine Optimization is a set of practices designed to improve the appearance and positioning of web pages in organic search results.
Servant leadership	A leadership style and philosophy whereby an individual interacts with others—either in a management or fellow employee capacity—to achieve authority rather than power.

Slack	A messaging app for business that connects people to the information they need.
SMB	Acronym for Small-to-Medium Business.
SWOT Analysis	A visual study tool that can be used to identify specific strengths and weaknesses in work and personal life situations. It helps with decision making and planning ahead.
Value Driver Tree	A graphical representation of the relationships between a company's financial statement items and its key value drivers.
Voice of Customers (VOC)	A term that describes customers' feedback about their experiences with and expectations for a company's products or services. It focuses on customer needs, expectations, understandings, and product improvement.

Authors

Eve Chen. B.B. MBA

A student and teacher of what makes companies achieve sustainable growth, Eve is an entrepreneur, veteran revenue marketer, and change driver with extensive experience from several global organizations. Driven by a relentless curiosity and a passion for excellence, Eve developed the first iteration of the Revenue Generation Value Chain (RVC) and a maturity framework in 2015 to guide organizations to transform into a high performing system with a methodical approach and align their resources to build a robust growth engine to exceed their goals. For the last 10 years she has headed up a revenue marketing and growth performance agency, The Growth Engine, which focuses on helping businesses of all sizes to accelerate their revenue results.

- Serial entrepreneur in both private and nonprofit sectors
- Expert revenue marketer and process optimizer
- Creator of Revenue Generation Value Chain (RVC), a growth acceleration framework
- Founder of The Growth Engine, a growth performance and revenue marketing consulting practice

- Former head of marketing for several multinationals in the technology space.
- Fluent in 5 languages. Market entry expert with experience in 26 countries.
- Led transformations for over 15 years for organizations ranging from innovative start-ups to Fortune 500s.
- Storyteller and Human 2 Human (H2H) expert
- Experienced coach for aspiring marketers

Connect with Eve at https://linkedin.com/in/evechen/

Ljubica Radoicic, MMkgt

A senior Marketing leader with 20 years of experience, Ljubica is customer-obsessed and focused on delivering best practice sales and marketing strategies to optimize teams and deliver growth. Ljubica's career spans global organizations across multiple industries including professional services, consulting, technology/SaaS, industrial, and construction (to name a few) where she led teams at a both functional and executive level. In these complex and challenging environments, she developed a unique ability to push past the tired strategies to deliver outstanding results and ROI. Using a creative and entrepreneurial flair to see and convert opportunity, Ljubica develops marketing and go-to-market strategies that capitalize on emerging opportunities, harnessing the latest marketing and digital trends to increase market share.

- B2B Sales & Marketing Evangelist
- Transformed marketing teams in 4 different organizations in APAC region
- Delivered growth of up to 177% YoY

- Set up marketing functions and teams in diverse regions (e.g., Greater China)
- Brand Strategy & Architecture SME
- Set up and managed BDR/SDR function
- CX & Customer Marketing Strategy Expert
- Speaker & Guest Lecturer (FHNW School of Business)

Connect with Ljubica at https://linkedin.com/in/ljubicaradoicic/

Brett Cowell MBA (Exec), B Com (Information Systems)

Brett spent two decades as a management consultant with several top-tier firms and working with leading global B2B and B2C clients across the world. During this time, he specialized in strategy and end-to-end performance improvement including operating model design and re-structuring, planning transformation (incl. Sales and Operations Planning), cross-functional alignment, Customer Service transformation/CRM, new product introduction, and performance management. He's worked across several industries including Technology and Telecommunications, Consumer Products/FMCG, Steel/Mining and Power & Utilities. In 2016 Brett founded Total Life Complete focusing on media, learning and experiences around Creativity, Leadership and Lifestyle. He teaches creativity and storytelling for leaders and entrepreneurs and runs the Brett Cowell Show podcast as well as several video shows around the "Complete" paradigm of living at a higher and deeper level at work and in life.

- Experienced/Expert Management Consultant strategy and business transformation (global B2B and B2C clients)

- Strategic Advisor
- Leadership/Business coach
- Creative Entrepreneur
- Immersive learning architect and lead trainer (in leadership and creativity)
- Author/Writer
- Video and Music Producer/DJ

Connect with Brett at: https://linkedin.com/in/brettcowell/

NOTES